SOME ETHICAL QUESTIONS OF PEACE AND WAR

WITH SPECIAL REFERENCE TO IRELAND

Rev. Walter McDonald, DD

with an Introduction by Tom Garvin

University College Dublin Press
Preas Choláiste Ollscoile Bhaile Átha Cliath

First published 1919

This edition first published by
University College Dublin Press, 1998

Introduction © Tom Garvin 1998

ISBN 1 900621 18 5
ISSN 1393–6883

University College Dublin Press
Newman House, St Stephen's Green, Dublin 2, Ireland

Cataloguing in Publication data available from the British Library

Typeset in Baskerville by Elaine Shiels, Bantry, Co. Cork
Printed in Ireland by Colour Books, Dublin

CONTENTS

PART I.—QUESTIONS OF PEACE

CHAPTER I

OF CERTAIN RECENT STATEMENTS MADE BY REPRESENTATIVE IRISH CATHOLICS; AND OF SOME QUESTIONS RAISED THEREBY

1. Ireland a Nation ?—2. The Mansion House Conference.—3. The Irish Parliamentary Party.—4. The Nationalist Section of the Convention.—5. Certain University Professors and Other Well-known People.—6. The Sinn Féin Clergy.—7. The Episcopal Body.—8. The Professor of Catholic Theology, National University.—9. A Maynooth Professor of Philosophy.—10. "The Irish Theological Quarterly". .... pp. 3–9

CHAPTER II

OF WHETHER IRELAND WAS EVER A UNITED AND FULLY INDEPENDENT NATION

1. Some Conditions of Nationhood.—2. Unity of Rule.—3. No such Unity in Ancient Ireland.—4. Independence of Leinster.— 5. The Kingdom of Ossory.—6. Analogy of the Holy See.—7. The British Colonies.—8. Late and Arrested Development .... pp. 10–16

CHAPTER III

OF WHETHER IRELAND EVER ACQUIESCED
IN LOSS OF INDEPENDENCE

CHAPTER IV

OF THE POSSIBILITY OF LOSS OF NATIONHOOD WITHOUT
ACQUIESCENCE; AND OF PRESCRIPTION BETWEEN NATIONS

CHAPTER V

OF THREE DEGREES OF CONQUEST; AND OF THE EFFICACY
OF FORCED CONSENT TO TRANSFER OF AUTHORITY

CHAPTER VI

OF THE EFFECT OF A TRANSFER OF JURISDICTION
SECURED BY CORRUPTION

CHAPTER VII

OF HOW A PEOPLE HITHERTO INDEPENDENT
MAY BE BOUND TO UNION WITH OTHERS;
AND OF HOW THIS MAY BE SECURED

CHAPTER VIII

OF SOME CONDITIONS OF COMPLETE SELF-DETERMINATION

CHAPTER IX

OF THE PRINCIPLE OF HOME RULE;
AND OF COLONIAL HOME RULE

CHAPTER X

OF MAJORITY RULE AND THE ULSTER QUESTION

CHAPTER XI

OF THE BASIS OF TAXATION; AND OF THE FINANCIAL RELATIONS BETWEEN GREAT BRITAIN AND IRELAND

NOTES

PART II.—QUESTIONS OF WAR

CHAPTER I

OF PREPARATION FOR WAR: CONSCRIPTION

CHAPTER II

OF CERTAIN CAUSES THAT JUSTIFY WAR

CHAPTER III

OF THE PRESSURE THAT MAY BE APPLIED
TO SECURE LOCAL SELF-GOVERNMENT

CHAPTER IV

OF THE CONDUCT OF WAR: (1) OF BOMBARDMENT
OF TOWNS, AND OF REPRISALS

CHAPTER V

OF THE CONDUCT OF WAR: (2) OF BLOCKADE

CHAPTER VI

OF THE CONDUCT OF WAR: (3) OF THE SUBMARINE

CHAPTER VII

OF SOME CONSEQUENCES OF WAR

APPENDIX

OF IRELAND SINCE THE UNION; AND OF THE PROSPERITY OF HOLLAND, DENMARK, AND OTHER SMALL NATIONS

INTRODUCTION
Tom Garvin

Walter McDonald
Biographical note

Walter McDonald was born in Mooncoin, County Kilkenny, in 1854. He came of farming stock and grew up in an Ireland recovering from the Great Famine. It was also an Ireland which was changing very rapidly: becoming English-speaking, literate, educated and post-feudal. It was becoming piously Catholic in an organised and bureaucratic way under the authoritarian leadership of Cardinal Paul Cullen. The Catholic Church, beloved of the general population although disliked by the British and Irish Protestant powers-that-were, was accumulating extensive cultural and political power under Cullen, first as Archbishop of Dublin and later as the first Irish Cardinal. A previously Irish-speaking peasant and farmer population was being transformed into an English-speaking and disciplined society of puritan yeoman farmers. Later this society was to decide that it wanted independence.

McDonald was ordained priest in 1876, and spent the rest of his life in teaching and administration at St Patrick's College, Maynooth and at the Dunboyne Establishment, the latter institution being in effect the graduate school of Maynooth Seminary. Maynooth had been financed by Catholic money after its founding in 1795, but it also needed British government tolerance to exist at its inception; at the time education of a Catholic kind was not quite illegal but was discouraged. Thereafter, British Government money financed Maynooth regularly, the purpose being to use Catholic priests to wean

Irish people from the revolutionary principles of the French Revolution. A curious alliance existed, in effect, between the Protestant British state in Ireland and the newly organised English-speaking Irish Catholic Church. London and Maynooth were united by a common terror of revolution, if by little else.

In McDonald's time, Maynooth was the most important Catholic seminary in the English-speaking world, and its intellectual character was to influence international English-speaking Catholicism for better or worse for two generations. Walter McDonald was therefore to have the potential—despite being personally a quiet and reclusive man—to shape the minds of Catholic priests directly or indirectly over five continents. He persistently tried to raise the intellectual level of the teaching staff at Dunboyne during his tenure.

He wrote a lot, and in 1906 he founded the *Irish Theological Quarterly*. He was unusually independent-minded by the standards of Catholic priests of his era, although always ultimately obedient to his beloved church. He was latterly quite a controversialist, and most of his written work came under the interdict of the official church authorities. His best-known works, published just before and just after his death in 1920, are *Some Ethical Questions of Peace and War* (1919) and *Reminiscences of a Maynooth Professor* (1925). Most of his other books and essays remained unpublished, or published in an edition of one copy, which amounts to the same thing. His book *Motion: Its Origin and Conservation* (1898) was ordered to be destroyed by the Catholic church, but copies have survived.

The ecclesiastical censors of his time regarded his philosophical views as perhaps brilliant, but possibly theologically unsound and certainly politically dangerous (among other things, he pointed out that priest academics often contradicted each other). He was never deprived of his chair, although, in despair, he occasionally considered giving it up. He spent his professional life being regarded as dangerously free in mentality by both some of the leaders of the Irish Catholic Church and by his superiors in Rome.

McDonald was a moderniser (as distinct from a Modernist), and believed that there was no necessary conflict between the doctrines of the Catholic system and the findings of modern Victorian science. He concerned himself particularly with raising the intellectual standards of the Irish Catholic church of his time. He was concerned by the tendency of senior clerics to behave in political life as propagandists and even demagogues rather than as learned and scrupulous men versed in the science of ethics. Concerning his attack, in his *Some Ethical Questions of Peace and War*, on the episcopal shift of political allegiance after the 1916 Rising and the conscription crisis of 1918, he wrote in his *Reminiscences of a Maynooth Professor*,

> I saw, with disgust, Irish Bishops, both here and in the United States and elsewhere, use claptrap phrases—about self-determination, rights of nations, government by consent, and other such catchwords—good enough for President Wilson or Mr Lloyd George, but unworthy of men who are supposed to have mastered the science of ethics as taught in our schools. In the use of these phrases, only too often in a sense which is false, our Bishops were competing for popular favour with political leaders: becoming, in fact, demagogues, while they should remain Bishops.[1]

On the theological side, his most important brush with ecclesiastical authority was *Motion*, written by him in the Dunboyne Institution in the early 1890s. This book was an attempt to rid Catholic theology of certain Aristotelian ideas and reconcile the Catholic *Weltanschauung* with the ideas of modern physics. Older ideas of direct divine intervention were still attractive to religious minds, but modern physics suggested that, if divine intervention occurred, it had occurred long ago, and the world had rolled along on its own without such intervention ever since, so far as anyone could make out. McDonald believed that there was no contradiction; the Blind Watchmaker could have a Minder.

1. Walter McDonald, *Reminiscences of a Maynooth Professor*, London, Jonathan Cape, 1925, 396. To caution readers: other editions are commonly defective. I am indebted to Dr Thomas O'Loughlin, University of Lampeter, for conversations and correspondence.

However, his colleagues and superiors in Ireland and, in particular, Rome concluded that his arguments were 'opposed to faith'.

> . . . I gathered that the complaint was, in substance, that my teaching was what is known in philosophy as Occasionalism— denial of true efficient causality to creatures, who are merely occasions of active interference on the part of God, to whom alone, as efficient cause, is to be ascribed whatever effect is produced.[2]

McDonald denied the accusation of occasionalism; he claimed to be able to reconcile the traditional Catholic doctrine of the independence of action with the equally traditional insistence on God's continuous production of vital action and everything else. His book was nonetheless held to be an attack on the doctrine of free will. The arguments in the book also had implications for Catholics' understanding of the scientific physics of the day. It may also be that he was simply far too bright, and was demonstrating that what powerful Catholic professors had taught in this area for many years was simply wrong. It appears also, however, that the real danger, as seen both in Ireland and in Rome, was the indirect implication of his ideas for the understanding of human conduct.[3]

McDonald's book was condemned, by a process which the author complained was secretive and was pervaded by a fear of public debate and free speech. The Catholic church, he felt, had 'got so much into the habit of these secret investigations' that it had come to look on public discussion as 'evil'. Such a political style, he argued, would permit no science to flourish and would stultify all investigation.[4] The Irish mind was to be darkened, he thought, by clerical obscurantism and intellectual cowardice. His book was prohibited by a secret decree of the Congregation of the Index in 1898, despite the fact that it had received an *Imprimatur* from the Archbishop of Dublin, William Walsh, and a *Nihil Obstat* from the *Censor Deputatus*.

2. Ibid., 115.
3. Ibid., 122.
4. Ibid., 127.

McDonald was clearly devastated by the condemnation, and this eventually drove him into a late and partial rebellion against the political subculture of Irish ecclesiastical Catholicism. Even at a mundane level, he had personally to ensure that copies of his book were withdrawn from bookshops and, eventually, that they be physically destroyed. Copies have, however, survived in university libraries and elsewhere, and I have been supplied with a copy *per viam occultam.*

McDonald was also involved in a celebrated case, that of Dr O'Hickey, holder of the chair of Irish at Maynooth. The Catholic bishops had opposed making the Irish language a core part of the curriculum of the new National University of Ireland, founded in 1908. This line was unpopular with many, and in particular with the newly politically mobilised younger generation of nationalists. O'Hickey, Douglas Hyde and Eoin MacNeill agitated in favour of compulsory Irish, thereby unintentionally but directly taking on the Catholic bishops. O'Hickey was dismissed from his chair, having refused to resign. McDonald took up O'Hickey's cause, which was appealed to Rome. However, the bishops succeeded in denying him a hearing.

The two books published in 1919 and 1925 reflected a long-delayed rebellion by a man who had obeyed an ecclesiastical system of thought control for most of his life because he was faithful to his religion and his church. The books represent an attempt at friendly and loyal criticism of an institution which he believed was endangering itself because of its hostility to freedom of thought, free speech and intellectual inquiry. His ultimate objection was to its implicit political theory, one of obedience to authority rather than to equality of opinions in the Greek or modern senses.

Some Ethical Questions of Peace and War

This little book is extraordinary in several ways. Firstly, it appeared in 1919, and therefore at a crucial historical juncture; it appeared just after an occasion (December, 1918) in which the Irish voters, goaded on by the apparent denial of Home Rule at the behest of the Ulster minority, the execution of the 1916 leaders and the extension of conscription to Ireland in April 1918, handed an electoral mandate for revolutionary independence to the Sinn Féin party. This popular revolution of feeling, involving the denial of the British right to govern Ireland, was aided and abetted by many Catholic priests, including some bishops. The delegitimation of the regime, which the events of 1912–19 entailed, was supported by much of the Catholic church. The church could be accused of following popular passion rather than trying to moderate and enlighten popular opinion, arguably the true function of a Christian priest.

Walter McDonald, already a sick man, was evidently horrified by this betrayal—as he saw it—of the legitimate British state in Ireland by the church. Whatever the ill-doings of the British state in Ireland—and he seems to have felt that they had been very much exaggerated by nationalist propagandists—that state's rule had been accepted as legitimate by the Catholic church for a very long time, and the great majority of people on the island, regardless of religion, had acquiesced in it loyally.

In the book he points out that Ireland had never been a united nation, independent and with its own state; that Irish tribal loyalties were stronger than any loyalty to Ireland; that the Irish tribes had long acquiesced in English, later British, rule; that legitimate authority can actually be derived from a conquest by force, as long as that conquest was sufficiently long ago; that taxation and conscription were logical consequences of legitimate government and that if Home Rule or self-determination were to be given to what he termed 'Celtic Ireland', then, logically, it had to be given to what he termed 'Saxon Ireland' too. Among other intriguing arguments, he suggested that the causes of Irish economic underdevelopment did not lie in the Union with Great Britain, as argued by separatist nationalists, but with the character of the Irish people themselves, who seemed unable to organise themselves for commerce in the way that Ulster people or English people of the period were. In the book he castigates those among the nationalists who argued that a German victory would mean Irish liberation; on the contrary, he felt, a German victory would mean the common ruin of both Britain and Ireland.

His opinions on many topics are now obsolete. What is important about McDonald is that he had the independence of mind to speak truth to power, and to an increasingly implacable power: the growing alliance of the Irish Catholic church and extreme popular nationalism. The reason he was able to do so, apart from personal courage, was that he was himself a priest of the Catholic church, and a man who sensed the end of his life was near. It is a terrible reflection on the period and on the tradition of Irish Catholic nationalism that it took a person of such status and of such detachment from the things of this world to come out in public with thoughts which many entertained privately, although usually in less coherent form. He was a Maynooth champion of freedom.

NOTE ON THE TEXT

The text of this edition is that of the original book published in London by Burns & Oates in 1919. It is complete and the author's own punctuation is retained

Walter McDonald
Photograph courtesy The Librarian, St Patrick's College, Maynooth

PREFACE

Most of the questions raised in this little book are new; at least in the sense that, as far as I know, they have not been dealt with hitherto in scientific fashion and on Catholic lines. We are not, however, left without guidance, of general principles; which need to be applied with caution to cases undreamt of, or certainly not investigated, by our fathers in the schools.

This has been attempted of late, in some cases; I doubt whether with sufficient detachment. The atmosphere is too full of passion, and will be for long. Our successors will see more clearly; and will make, for all sides, allowances too generous for such as have lived through these last dreadful years.

And yet, as the whole world is talking of these questions, the Catholic schools of ethics should not ignore them. Not that on any of them one can hope to say the last word; but that, surveying them from different angles, one may direct attention to aspects that might be overlooked, and so contribute to a fuller view and a more equitable decision.

As some of the opinions here advanced run counter to the feelings of many Irishmen, I deem it well to say, that, should it come to boasting,—as St. Paul wrote, in like circumstances, when he had something unpalatable to tell his countrymen,— few can show a strain of Gaelic blood more ancient and pure than mine. According to Professor MacNeill, Ossory was a pre-Milesian kingdom; while Iverk in Ossory, to which I belong, he identifies with the Lagin des Gabair, a still more ancient people.

To judge from the recorded lists of princes of both territories, Domnal was a common name therein, at the time when such names became surnames. It still clings to a hill and a glen in Iverk. And as for the women of my ancestry, as far as they can be traced, not one of them bore a non-Irish maiden name. My Christian name, however, indicates that there was a mixture somewhere.

Of my forbears, moreover, none, as far as I can learn, ever took service of any kind under the English, or got any special favour from them. Whatever pay they received was the price of farm produce; and came ultimately, to them as to their neighbours, then as now, from Britain. In that sense I was brought up on British gold, and should deem it shame not to recognise the obligation. Otherwise I owe England nothing, except fair play; nor have I the least hope, or desire, of any special favour from her.

To my own people, of the Gael, is due the best I have: truth; if, indeed, I have it. A little south of Iverk, among the Deisi, there is a proverb,—first uttered, folk say, by a rock that split in delivery:—Truth is bitter. Like other bitter things, it is wholesome: in politics and economics, as in things spiritual, it and it alone makes us free.

Walter McDonald

SOME ETHICAL QUESTIONS OF PEACE AND WAR

WITH SPECIAL REFERENCE TO IRELAND

PART I

Questions of Peace

CHAPTER I

OF CERTAIN RECENT STATEMENTS MADE BY REPRESENTATIVE IRISH CATHOLICS; AND OF SOME QUESTIONS RAISED THEREBY

1. *IRELAND a Nation?*—Some time ago a group of priests, of whom the writer was one, were conversing on Irish politics. The question of union with Great Britain arose; and when I remarked that Ireland is part of a United Kingdom, and, as such, bound to contribute her fair share, in treasure and military service, to the support and defence of the whole, one of the party annihilated me with the question, more than once repeated: "Are we not a nation?" It was his only argument; but it satisfied him.

2. *The Mansion House Conference.—When,* in the spring of 1918, the Imperial Government proposed to make military service compulsory in Ireland, there was held in the Mansion House, Dublin, a notable conference of lay leaders of the different sections of Nationalists. A report of the proceedings appeared in the Dublin newspapers of April 19, wherein we were told that "the Conference adopted the following Declaration:—

"Taking our stand on Ireland's separate and distinct nationhood, and affirming the principle of liberty, that the Governments of Nations derive their just powers from the consent of the governed, we deny the right of the British Government, or any external authority, to impose compulsory service on Ireland against the clearly expressed will of the Irish people. The passing of the Conscription Bill by the British House of Commons must be regarded as a declaration of war on the Irish Nation. . . . It is in direct violation of the right of small nationalities to self-determination; which even the Prime

Minister of England . . . himself announced as an essential condition for peace at the Peace Conference".

Of those who signed the foregoing we know that Messrs. De Valera and Griffith hold that Ireland is a nation in the sense of being fully independent, at least *de iure*. And, of course, if this were so, it would completely justify the opposition of Irishmen to the Conscription Act. But is it Mr. Dillon's view, or Mr. Devlin's, who also signed the Declaration ? Or is it in that sense Mr. Healy, K.C., another of the signatories, calls Ireland a nation ?

3. *The Irish Parliamentary Party.*—On April 20,—two days after the Mansion House Conference,—the Irish Parliamentary Party met in Dublin, and passed the following resolution:—"That the enforcement of compulsory military service on a Nation, without its consent, constitutes one of the most brutal acts of tyranny and oppression that any government can be guilty of. That the present proposal of Mr. Lloyd George's government, to enforce conscription on Ireland, is an outrage and a gross violation of the national right of Ireland". This was repeated, by the same Party, at another meeting held in Dublin on May 17 following.

Now all these gentlemen, on being introduced to the British House of Commons,—some of them many times,—had taken an oath of allegiance to the Imperial Government. One wonders what did they mean. It cannot be that they have seen the error of their ways and would not take such an oath now; for they complain of the Sinn Féin Party for not allowing Irish Members of Parliament to sit at Westminster.

4. *The Nationalist Section of the Convention.*— At the recent Convention, the Nationalist section, including a number of Members of Parliament and some Bishops, agreed that "notwithstanding the establishment of an Irish Parliament, or anything contained in the Government of Ireland Act, the supreme power and authority of the Parliament of the United Kingdom shall remain unaffected and undiminished, over all persons, matters, and things in Ireland and every part thereof". Ireland a Nation, in this sense, does not mean Ireland completely independent. In what sense, one wonders,

is it a nation to the minds of those members of the Convention ?

5. *Certain University Professors and Other Well-known People.*— On May 18, 1918, there appeared in "The Freeman's Journal" a statement drawn up by certain well-known people,— leaders of thought, presumedly,—including Mrs. A. S. Green, and Professors Hyde, Magennis, and O'Sullivan, of the National University. They affirmed that "the decision of the Parliament of the British People to conscribe the manhood of Ireland,— by an order of the English Privy Council,—in thus deliberately ignoring our national status, denies it. . . . The treatment which shall be meted out to a small nation, one of the most ancient, affords a crucial test of the sincerity of any Power's adhesion to the cause of world freedom and the rights of nations". Did the Professors, I wonder, mean to affirm that Ireland is completely independent, owing no allegiance to the Parliament of the United Kingdom?

6. *The Sinn Féin Clergy.*—At the late parliamentary election it was the foremost plank in the Sinn Féin platform that Ireland is *de iure* a completely independent nation; and the candidates of the party pledged themselves, if elected, to make it their first business to secure this right. The Dáil Éireann, which resulted, and which met in Dublin on Jan. 21, 1919, issued a "Declaration of Independence", which was suppressed by the Censor. The substance of the Declaration, I take it, may be gathered from a published "Message to the Free Nations", which contains the following:—"Nationally, the race, the language, the customs, and the conditions of Ireland, are radically distinct from the English. Ireland is one of the most ancient nations in Europe, and she has preserved her national integrity, vigorous and intact, through seven centuries of foreign oppression. She has never relinquished her national rights, and throughout the long era of English usurpation, she has in every generation defiantly proclaimed her inalienable right of nationhood, down to the last glorious resort to arms in 1916".

Great numbers of the junior clergy, and a considerable body of their seniors, with some even of the Bishops, supported the Sinn Féin candidates, or voted for them. Some of this, I know, was bluff—asking, as I have heard one man put it, for more than they hoped to get. Others voted Sinn Féin as for the less of two evils. But many of the priests, and perhaps some of the Bishops, seem to have acted on the conviction that Ireland is *de iure* a fully independent nation. Is this really their teaching?

7. *The Episcopal Body.*—In the same issue of the Dublin newspapers that contained the Report of the Mansion House Conference, already quoted, there appeared, side by side with that document, a Statement of the Archbishops and Bishops of Ireland, wherein their Lordships complained that "an attempt is being made to force conscription upon Ireland against the will of the Irish nation. Which would seem to imply that, to the mind of the Bishops, Ireland is not bound by any Act of the Imperial Parliament which may have been passed against the vote of a majority of the Irish Members. Is this, I wonder, a fair inference from their Lordships' statement? Is it their teaching?

8. *The Professor of Catholic Theology, National University.*—The statement of the Bishops was published on April 19; and on the 14th of next month,—when, perhaps, maturer reflection had suggested the advisability of some defence based on scientific principles,—there appeared in the Dublin newspapers an article on "The Theology of Resistance", signed "P. Finlay, Professor of Catholic Theology, National University of Ireland". In this article Father Finlay said:—"They [Irish Catholics, with rare exceptions] deny that compulsory military service may ever be imposed by one people upon another; and they claim that Ireland is a distinct people from Great Britain. This was evidently in the Bishops' mind when they wrote: 'An attempt is being made to force conscription upon Ireland against the will of the Irish nation'. It is useless and unnecessary to discuss what constitutes a nation. Whatever it may be—natural boundaries, mentality, religious sympathies, history, race,—it divides and always has divided Ireland from Great Britain. . . . There are links which unite us; but they are as nothing when compared with the facts which keep us apart.

We are far less one with Great Britain than are any of her colonies,—Canada, South Africa, New Zealand, or Australia".

Professor Finlay repeated this—more deliberately, if possible,— a month later, and almost in the same words, in the Jesuit Quarterly, "Studies". His principle,—that compulsory military service may never be imposed by one people upon another,—holds, plainly, of fully independent peoples. It did not take a University Professor of Theology to teach even plain folk that. But what if such a law were passed by a Parliament common to both? "Irish Catholics", he says, "do not deny generally the right of a London Parliament to make laws for Ireland"; nor, I take it, to impose taxes. It may be, indeed, that while a parliament common to two peoples may legislate for and tax either without their consent, it may not exact compulsory military service. Is this, one wonders, the position?

9. *A Maynooth Professor of Philosophy.*—In June 1918 "The Irish Ecclesiastical Record" published an article under the title of "The Conscription Menace in Ireland and Some Issues Raised by It". The article was signed by Dr. Coffey, Professor of Philosophy in Maynooth College; who indicated three lines on which resistance to conscription was likely to be justified. Some would admit the right of the Westminster Parliament to make ordinary laws and impose ordinary taxes, but not the Blood Tax. Others would "justly appeal" to certain historical facts, connected with the Act of Union and what has happened since, "for the purpose of proving that no law of the Imperial Parliament is directly binding on Irishmen". This line of argument "goes deeper than the first; and suggests yet a third which goes deeper still. It is briefly this: that England possesses no moral right to conscript Irishmen, for the simple reason that England has not now, and *never has had*, [italics in original] any moral right to rule or govern Ireland".

This is plain speaking; and as it appeared in a monthly ecclesiastical journal which boasts that it is published under episcopal sanction, while the article was signed by a Professor in a seminary of which the Bishops of Ireland are Trustees, one can hardly be blamed for taking it that the teaching, if not that of their Lordships, is not any way discountenanced by them. It would not, I fancy, have pleased Cardinal Cullen; but things may have changed since his time.

10. *"The Irish Theological Quarterly."*—In the following month of July the Editors of "The Irish Theological Quarterly" published a number of unsigned Notes,—editorial comments, plainly,—wherein they say that "among the war—aims of the Allies, clearly and strongly asserted by all of them, we find the independence of small nations: can anyone in his senses deny that, among the small nations, Ireland, the oldest of them all, except Greece, has a claim as good as any and better than most? "Now, Holland and Switzerland are completely independent; and as Ireland has a better claim than either, she, too, must be fully independent *de iure*. One would think that this was plain to anyone in his senses"; and yet the writer of these Notes had his doubts—or, at least, apprehensions.

For he called to mind the official teaching of the Holy See to the effect that members of the Fenian Brotherhood are excommunicated, for plotting against a legitimate government. But the authority against which they plot is the present government of Ireland; which, therefore, must be held legitimate, by all who accept the official teaching of the Holy See. One wonders whether it also has suffered change.

In view of all this, it seems time for Irish Catholics to ask themselves,—many of them must be asking,—what is the teaching of the Bishops, priests, schools of Theology, Philosophy, Canon Law, of Rome itself, as to the binding force of laws made by the present *de facto* rulers of our country? Is it true that, as Dr. Coffey has suggested, the Parliament of Westminster has not and never had any moral right to govern us?

His argument,—which seems to represent the mind of Sinn Féin,—may be reduced to the following syllogism—No fully independent nation ceases to be so *de iure*, except by the free consent of its people; but Ireland was at one time a nation fully independent, while its people never freely consented to resign that status; therefore she is *de iure* fully independent now.

Here we have as major premiss what purports to be a universal principle of Ethics; particularised in the minor by two statements of fact. And although, perhaps, criticism should begin with the major, as to which alone I can claim any special competence, I will ask the reader's forbearance while I deal with the statements of fact in the first place; under promise of criticising the ethical principle in due course.

CHAPTER II

OF WHETHER IRELAND WAS EVER A
UNITED AND FULLY INDEPENDENT NATION

1. *SOME Conditions of Nationhood*—Father Finlay,—who, like so many others, justifies Ireland's resistance to conscription on the ground that she is a nation, and, as such, may not, without injustice, be forced into military service against her will,—declines to be drawn into a discussion as to what constitutes a nation. He mentions, as likely constituents, "natural boundaries, mentality, religious sympathies, history, race"; but omits what some may deem still more important—the unity that derives from common rule. For lack of which, Ireland, possibly, may not have been a nation in any strict sense, till it was united by England; when it would lack another no less important constituent—complete self-government. So that, instead of being the most ancient small nation of Europe, except Greece, as the writer in "The Theological Quarterly" represents her, our country would never have been a nation at all. That is, if unity of rule and independence are requisites of nationhood.

2. *Unity of Rule.*—Take unity of rule. It can be maintained, I think, with some show of reason, that, despite natural boundaries, distinctive mentality, religious sympathies, history, race, and so on, Greece in the time of Pericles was not a united nation; nor Italy, while Rome was under the kings, or in the sixteenth century; nor Great Britain, in the time of the Confessor nor England under the Heptarchy; nor Germany immediately before the Franco-Prussian war nor the Indian tribes of North America at the coming of the "Mayflower". Those among us who are growing old have seen two nations formed: Germany and Italy.

   3. No such Unity in Ancient Ireland.—Turning now to the
history of our own country, I read:— "In pagan times Ireland
must not be regarded as one kingdom, governed by one king
and one common system of laws; it was rather a confederation
of small states or clans, each making its own laws, raising and
spending its own taxes, governed by its own chieftain, and
practically independent within its own limits. There was an
Ardri, who ruled at Tara; and who, amongst the various
princes, was first in dignity; but whose authority over these
princes—and he claimed some,—was shadowy and nominal,
and frequently his authority was flouted and his person and
office despised".[1] The position must have been not unlike that
which Protestants are so willing to accord the Roman Pontiff
in Church matters; which, Catholics strongly insist, would not
make for anything like real unity of government.

   This was in pagan times,—before the coming of St. Patrick,—
when, according to Professor MacNeill, the latest and best
authority, there was not even a shadowy High-King in Erin.
"It is almost certain", he writes,[2] "that the high-kingship dates
no further back than Niall of the Nine Hostages (end of the
fourth century), in whose descendants it was vested till the time
of Brian Boramha, A.D. 1002". "Niall, founder of the O'Neill
dynasty of Tara, was king of Meath at the time of the captivity
[of St. Patrick]. He is the first person who can possibly be
recognised as King of All Ireland. If the high-kingship existed
in his time, it was a novelty".[3]

   Whenever it began, and as long as it continued, it seems to
have been only the "shadowy and nominal" thing described by
Dr. D'Alton; flouted often in the person of the monarch, and
despised in his office. Mr. MacNeill, in one place, represents
it as an hegemony:—"The Book of Rights, judged by inter-
nal evidence, was composed at a time when the Kingdom of
Cashel was putting forward claims to the hegemony, or, as
it is commonly called, the monarchy of Ireland".[4] We know

---

[1] D'Alton, *History of Ireland,* i. 19.
[2] "New Ireland Review", xxv. p.18.
[3] *Ibid.* p. 331.
[4] *Ibid.* p. 65.

what hegemony meant in Ancient Greece; and how little it served to make the Greek States a united nation. Spain had at one time an hegemony in Europe; which passed, in turn, to Austria, France, England, Germany; without ever welding the nations of Europe into one. The United States has long had an hegemony in America, with a kind of sovereign authority represented by the Monroe doctrine. Yet there are, I believe, more than thirty fully independent nations on the American continent.

"The high-kingship", says Mr. MacNeill, in another lecture, "was not an institution of such efficient unity as to inspire greatness of literary design throughout the nation. In the early historical period, the supremacy [hegemony, once more] waved irregularly among four great branches of the race of Niall. But from the middle of the eighth century it steadied down to a regular and recognised alternation between the princes of Cinel Eogain and Clann Cholmain. The new status did not visibly affect the nation at large. The provincial kings gave hostages when they must, and refused them when they dared".

So, again, Arthur Ua Clerigh, who seems to have made a critical study of the history of our country:—"The Gael remained a clansman when he ought to have been a patriot, and Erin continued to be a 'trembling sod' when it ought to have become a homogeneous and harmonious nation". "We do not attach very great importance to the *Book of Rights*. It was evidently composed, or thoroughly recast, about the time of Cormac mac Cuilenainn [A.D. 900], and is intended to magnify and exalt Cashel in a secular and religious point of view. Whatever value the book may have as regards the provincial kings, as regards the Ard-Righ it seems to indicate that, at any rate in times of peace, he had no rights except the right of Visitation and Refection".[5] "The frequent raids made by the Ard-Righ, not only to lift the boromba but to enforce tribute from every part of Erin, plainly show that, whatever his right may have been, his claims were much more extensive". "The contest [for the overlordship] was renewed again, this

[5] "New Ireland Review", xxv. p. 336.

time between the O'Connor of Conacht and the O'Lochlainns of Aileach. Turlough O'Connor . . . crushed the Munster men. But, being attacked in the same year by Muirchertach Ua Lochlainn, he was forced to give him hostages. He renewed the struggle, however, the following year, and maintained it till his death, in 1056. The latter was not in position to establish his claim to the shadowy overlordship".[6] Note the recurrence of Dr. D'Alton's term, "shadowy".

4. *Independence of Leinster.*—The High King, it seems, made considerable claims to tribute; which, however, were not admitted by the sub-kings, who gave only what they were not in position to refuse. Let us hear Dr. Joyce:—

"He [the High-King, Tuathal] imposed on Leinster an enormous tribute, called the Boruma or Boru, to be paid to the Kings of Ireland every second year. The tribute was never yielded without resistance more or less, and for many centuries it was the cause of constant bloodshed". "Laeghaire [Leary], the son of Niall, succeeded in 428. In the fifth year of his reign St. Patrick came to Ireland on his great mission. This king, like many of his predecessors, waged war against the Leinstermen, to exact the Boru tribute; but they defeated him and took him prisoner. Then they made him swear by the sun and wind and all the elements that he would never again demand the tribute; and when he had sworn, they set him free". "The Irish kings continued to exact the Boru tribute from the Leinstermen, who struggled manfully against it to the last. But at the earnest solicitation of St. Moling, Finaghta the Festive, who became king in 674, renounced the Boru for himself and his successors".[7]

5. *The Kingdom of Ossory.*—Among those who were subjected to and resisted the claim for tribute were the people of Ossory; who, according to Professor MacNeill, were "neither tributary nor subordinate to any of the Irish provincial kings down to the time of the Book of Rights (900 or 1000 A.D.), and acknowledged no suzerainty, except the somewhat shadowy overlordship—as far as southern Ireland was concerned—of

[6] *History of Ireland to the Coming of Henry II.*, pp. 76, 263, 389.
[7] *A Concise History of Ireland*, pp. 41, 44, 53.

the over-kings of Meath".[8] Note once more, the recurrence of the term "shadowy".

What allegiance the men of Ossory thought they owed the high-king, Brian,—who went nearest of all to consolidating the clans,—appears from the onslaught they made on his battered forces returning from Clontarf. It may seem unpatriotic, to one of wider vision; but they saw in Brian only a Milesian tyrant, who derived his surname, of Boru, from the efficacy with which he lifted the hateful tribute; which they, an independent people, had steadfastly refused. "Ossory was an independent and unsubdued Pre-Milesian state throughout the entire historical period, down to the Norman invasion. Upper Ossory retained its independent and its native rulers till the time of the English confiscation by Queen Mary, and even later; and was thus the longest established Celtic principality in the world, with an unbroken history under its own princes of at least 1,200 years".[9]

These are some of the facts: a sample merely. They show a number of clans, more or less dependent on provincial kings, and under a high-king whose authority all these writers represent as "shadowy". Was it sufficient to bind these warring clans into anything like a real nation? Mr. T. W. Rolleston, in a Note to an article on St. Patrick, writes:—"The ecclesiastical 'Cursing of Tara' in the sixth century ended all chance of establishing a central monarchy with an effective military system in Ireland".[10]

6. *Analogy of the Holy See.*—During great part of the time while this struggle was going on, another over-lordship was being exercised; that which the Roman Pontiffs claimed over western Europe, in virtue of a donation of the Emperor Constantine, now recognised as fictitious. Apart, however, from this donation, kings in different countries swore allegiance to the Pope, making him their suzerain, with a right to tribute. In England, for instance, John, "of his own free will, and with the unanimous consent of his barons", as his charter states,

---

[8] "New Ireland Review", xxv. p.76.
[9] "New Ireland Review", xxv. p. 77.
[10] "Nineteenth Century", April 1919, p. 757.

granted to Pope Innocent and Innocent's rightful successors, "the Kingdom of England and the Kingdom of Ireland, to be holden by himself and the heirs of his body of the Bishop of Rome in fee, by the annual rent of one thousand marks . . . He then took, in the usual manner, an oath of fealty to the Pope; the very same oath which vassals took to their lords".[11] This, not so very shadowy, suzerainty did not make England a mere province of a greater European nation ruled by the Pope. Much less, I fancy, did the men of Ossory regard themselves as a province of an Irish nation ruled by king Brian.

7. *The British Colonies.*—It may be said, I know, that the colonies of Britain form one nation with the mother country; though they pay no tribute, and would fly to arms, as did those of New England, if it were demanded; and though they recognise no common bond of rule more substantial than the shadowy overlordship of the high-kings of Erin.

But, surely, Australia is not one nation with England in anything like the sense in which England herself is one; or as England, Scotland, and Wales are now the British Nation. It is but a weak bond, perhaps, that unites the colonies to the mother country; and it would break, no doubt, if subjected to strain. The strain, however, has not come, so far; with the result that the bond, feeble as it is, continues. In the case of the Irish clans there was constant tension—internecine war; and we are asked to believe that, whereas one such quarrel, over a tax on tea, separated her American colonies from England; as anything of the kind would separate Canada, S. Africa, or Australia to-morrow; Leinster remained united with Tara or Cashel after warring with them in succession, over the boru tribute, for several hundred years.

8. *Late and Arrested Development.*—The truth seems to be that, during all these centuries of intertribal warfare, the Irish clans were struggling towards national unity, just like their neighbours in England, France, and elsewhere; with the difference, unfortunately, that whereas unity was achieved across the Channel, with us no native power grew strong enough to

[11]Lingard, *History of England*, ii. p 165.

overbear the self-will of the chiefs; till, too late for nationhood, the clans were welded together and reduced to subjection by the Norman English. This, if not the truth, is so like it as to call for evidence to the contrary from those who base Ireland's claim to independence on the fact that she is the most ancient nation in Europe, except Greece. May it be that neither Ancient Greece nor Ancient Ireland was one nation, but many? If, indeed, we may call such States as Athens and Ossory nations. A "principality" we have just heard Ossory designated by Professor MacNeill.

CHAPTER III

OF WHETHER IRELAND EVER ACQUIESCED
IN LOSS OF INDEPENDENCE

1. *TWO Periods of Irish History.*—The second statement of fact contained in the minor premiss of Dr. Coffey's argument, is to the effect that Ireland never freely resigned her status as a fully independent nation. I find it hard to harmonise this with certain incidents in the history of our country.

Irish history, from the coming of the Normans is divided by Dr. Coffey into two periods; the earlier from the landing of Strongbow to the Act of Union with Great Britain, in 1800; the later from the Union to the present day. During pre-Union times there was no question of submission except to the King of England not to any Imperial Parliament. What Parliament there was, to rule us, was Irish—of some kind; at least Anglo-Irish, Cromwellian, or Williamite. From the Union, if we submitted, it was to the King and the Parliament of Westminster.

2. *Henry II.*—In the first period we are told that Henry II., almost on his arrival, in 1171, was met, at Waterford, "by Dermot MacCarthy, King of Desmond, who was the first Irish prince to submit and pay tribute. . . . Henry next marched by Lismore to Cashel, where he received the submission of Donall O'Brien of Limerick, and of many others of the southern princes. After this he returned to Waterford; and having taken possession of Wexford, he proceeded to Dublin, where he was received in great state. Here he was visited by most of the other Irish princes, all of whom submitted to him. Roderick O'Connor [the High King] did not come, but he sent his submission. The Irish princes and nobles were invited to spend the Christmas with the King in Dublin; and they

were astonished at the magnificence of the display, and much pleased with the attention shown to themselves".[1]

Four years later, Roderick, the High King, "finding that he could not prevent the daily incursions of the English raiders, determined to claim the protection of King Henry. Accordingly, he sent three ambassadors to England, one of whom was Archbishop Laurence O'Toole, and a treaty was arranged between the two kings. Under this treaty, which was signed at Windsor in 1175, it was agreed that Roderick was to remain king of Connaught, which he was to hold directly as vassal to Henry; that he was to rule the rest of Ireland as vassal, except the portions held by the English colony; and that through him the other Irish Kings and chieftains were to pay tribute to King Henry".[2]

3. Richard II.—Two centuries passed, and in the reign of Richard II. and the time of Art MacMurrogh, "the Irish chiefs saw that submission was inevitable. At a place called Ballygorey, near Carlow, Mowbray Earl of Nottingham received the submission of a number of the southern chiefs, in 1395; and amongst them Art MacMurrogh, the most dreaded of all. The King himself received the northern chiefs at Drogheda. Altogether about seventy-five chiefs submitted to the King and to Mowbray. They were afterwards invited to Dublin, where they were feasted sumptuously for several days by the King, who knighted the four provincial kings: O'Neill of Ulster; O'Connor of Connaught; MacMurrogh of Leinster; and O'Brien of Thomond. . . . As for the submission and reconciliation of the Irish chiefs, it was all pure sham. They did not look upon King Richard as their lawful sovereign; and as the promises they made had been extorted by force, they did not consider themselves bound to keep them".[3] Not the first "scrap of paper", I suppose.

4. The Tudors.—Passing on to the reign of Henry VIII., we find that "the Irish chiefs showed a general disposition for

---

[1] Joyce, *Concise History,* pp. 85-86.
[2] Ibid p. 88.
[3] Joyce, *Concise History,* p. 110,

peace". The Lord Deputy, St. Leger, "took full advantage of their pacific mood, and by skilful management induced them to submit. They all acknowledged the King's temporal and spiritual authority. . . . It was resolved to confer on Henry the title of King of Ireland. With this object a parliament was assembled in Dublin on the 12th June, 1541; and in order to lend greater importance to its decisions, a number of the leading Irish chiefs were invited to attend it. The Act conferring the title of King of Ireland on Henry and his successors was passed through both Houses rapidly and with perfect unanimity. Titles were conferred on many of the chiefs. Conn Bacach O'Neill was made Earl of Tyrone, and his (reputed) son, Ferderagh or Matthew, was made Baron of Dungannon, with right to succeed as Earl of Tyrone. O'Brien was made Earl of Thomond; and MacWilliam Burke, who is commonly known as Ulick-na-gann, was made Earl of Clanrickard. O'Donnell was promised to be made Earl of Tyrconnell; but the title was not actually conferred till a considerable time after".[4]

5. *Great Chiefs Become Earls.*—One of the most touching incidents in Irish history is what is called the Flight of the Earls— of Tyrone and Tyrconnell; no longer O'Neill and O'Donnell. The Earldom was a badge of submission: of the chiefs, and, through them, of the whole of Gaelic Ulster. Connaught, at the same period, was under the sway of another earl, Clanrickard; Munster under three: Desmond, Thomond, and Ormond; Leinster under Kildare, Ormond, and MacMurrogh. All recognised as their liege the King of England, against whose arbitrary rule the people of England were soon to rebel.

6. *The Stuarts.*—"James I. was the first English king who was universally acknowledged by the Irish as their lawful sovereign".[5]

The Confederation of Kilkenny has some claim to speak for a united Ireland; yet its motto was *Pro Deo, Rege, Patria, Hiberni Unanimes;* the king being the Stuart King of England.

---

[4] Joyce, *Concise History*, pp. 134–5.
[5] Joyce, *Ibid.* p. 184.

At a conference of the clergy of the nation held at Kilkenny in 1642, it was declared that "the war which Catholics in Ireland are now waging against sectaries, mainly Puritans, for the defence of the Catholic religion, for the conservation of the prerogatives and royal rights of our Most Serene King Charles, . . . is just and lawful". The prelates "summoned a General Assembly, to consist of representatives elected by the Catholic Confederates in all the counties and important towns". It "met in Kilkenny on the 24th October, 1642. Father Meehan writes:—'On that day the representatives of the Irish Catholics, deputed by the cities, counties, and towns, were assembling in the City of Kilkenny. . . . It was a grand and solemn spectacle; nor does the history of any country record a more spirit-stirring scene' ".[6] Among the decrees of this National Assembly, published by Cardinal Moran,[7] we read:—"All the inhabitants of Ireland and each of them shall be most faithful to our Sovereign Lord the King, his heires and lawfull successors and shall maintaine, to the utmost of their power his royall prerogatives, against his enemies". His enemies were the Parliament of England.

Some years later, when the Confederates divided, and Owen Roe O'Neill had been denounced by the Supreme Council as an enemy, a rebel, and a traitor, that representative Irishman issued a proclamation which concludes thus:—"We conjure all Confederate Catholics to co-operate with us against all factionaries who, despite the oath of association, support rebels, to the prejudice of his Majesty".[8]

In less than fifty years after this another assembly, truly national, met in Dublin; "The Patriot Parliament of 1689", as it is styled by Duffy; and as to which Davis writes that it was the first and last which ever sat in Ireland since the English invasion, possessed of national authority, and complete in all its parts. The King, by law and in fact—the King who, by his Scottish descent, his creed, and his misfortunes, was dear

[6] Carrigan, *History of the Diocese of Ossory*, iii. p.20.
[7] *Spicilegium Ossoriense*, ii. p.9.
[8] *Carrigan, Ibid.* p.30.

(mistakenly or not) to the majority of the then people of Ireland,—presided in person over that Parliament. The Peerage consisted it of the best blood, Milesian and Norman, of great wealth and of various creeds. The Commons represented the Irish Septs, the Danish towns, and the Anglo-Irish counties and boroughs. No parliament of equal rank, from King to Commons, sat here since; none sat here before or since so national in composition and conduct".[9]

Its very first Act was one of recognition of the sovereignty of James II., King of England.[10]

7. *The Repeal Movement.*—In the second period of our history, from the Union to the present day, one notes three leading movements: (1) for Repeal of the Union, under O'Connell; (2) for complete independence, under the Fenians; and (3) for Home Rule, under Butt, Parnell, and Redmond.

It may be argued, I think, with fair show of reason, that O'Connell recognised the Union as valid, and the Parliament of Westminster as having jurisdiction over Ireland. Not a few Sinn Féiners, if I do not mistake, assume that to sit in that Parliament, as O'Connell did, implies such an admission; which I think reasonable. Those who sit there take an oath of allegiance to the Sovereign, who has no authority apart from the Westminster Parliament; so that the oath implies recognition of that body as being empowered to rule, with the King.

Now consider what O'Connell did when first elected, before Emancipation. "On the oath of abjuration being tendered to him, he read over audibly these words—'that the sacrifice of the Mass, and the invocation of the Blessed Virgin Mary and other saints, as now practised in the Church of Rome, are impious and idolatrous'. At the subsequent passage, relatively to the falsely imputed Catholic doctrine of the dispensing power of the Pope, he again read aloud, and paused. Then, slightly raising his voice, he bowed, and added: 'I decline, Mr. Clerk, to take this oath. Part of it I know to be

---

[9] *The Patriot Parliament of 1689*, p. 39. Ed. by Sir C. G. Duffy, in *The New Irish Library.*

[10] *The Patriot Parliament of 1689*, p. 43.

false another part I do not believe to be true'".[11] Had he regarded as unfounded and untrue the claim of the King and Parliament to make laws for Ireland, he would have been bound to treat the oath of allegiance to the Sovereign in the same manner.

No doubt he proclaimed his intention of doing all in his power, within the constitution, to secure Repeal of the Act of Union. This, however, may be understood in the sense of forcing Parliament to renounce authority which it possessed, but which had been acquired inequitably and was unfair towards Ireland. Catholic ethics supplies many examples of pressure legitimately applied to secure renunciation of a right that is held validly, though inequitably acquired.[12]

8. *The Fenian Brotherhood.*—Well, the Repeal agitation gave way to one for complete independence, initiated by the Young Irelanders and continued by the Fenians. The new movement had the sympathy of the people; but sympathy only of an inefficacious kind: *secundum quid,* as we say in Moral Theology. They would like to support the Fenians, if they could do so without peril to soul or body; but the religious guides, whom they feared and trusted much more than they did the Fenian leaders, assured and convinced them that it was criminal to become enrolled as a member of the Fenian Brotherhood. This extinguished Fenianism.

It was then, and still is, part of the Common Law of the Catholic Church, promulgated anew recently in every diocese in Ireland, that "those who get enrolled in the Masonic Sect, or any other such association which plots against the Church or legitimate civil powers, incurs excommunication *ipso facto*". The canon is taken, with a slight verbal change, from the Constitution *Apostolicae Sedis,* promulgated in October 1869; while on June 12, 1870, the S. Congregation of the Holy Office, or Roman Inquisition, published a decree to the effect that the Fenian Brotherhood was comprised under the censure. As a consequence, Catholic members of that society could not

---

[11] D'Arcy McGee, *History of Ireland,* Book xii., Ch. viii.

[12] See my tractate on *Some Aspects of the Social Question,* Book i.

get the sacraments from any Irish priest, or be buried with Church rites, if they died unrepentant. This caused the Fenian spirit to evaporate.

Accordingly, the authorities of the Church in Ireland taught officially,—enforcing the teaching with the severest penalties at their disposal,—that the government against which the Fenians plotted was legitimate; and the Irish Catholic laity cried Amen; reluctantly, no doubt; but they contrived to say it.

9. *The Home Rule Movement.*—After this they resumed O'Connell's method, of constitutional agitation; with a change of object no longer pressing for Repeal, but only for Home Rule. The change is significant; meaning that those who took part in the new movement,—and they were, practically, the entire Catholic body,—recognised the right of the Imperial Parliament to rule Ireland in matters imperial. This was acknowledged implicitly, by the nature of the movement, as distinguished from that for Repeal; and even explicitly, in ever so many speeches, delivered both inside and outside the House of Commons at Westminster by the Irish leaders; who protested that the movement was not for separation, as the Unionists contended, but only for Irish control of purely Irish affairs.

Hence I say first, that Home Rule, as distinguished from Repeal, meant recognition of the jurisdiction of the Parliament of Westminster in all imperial matters; and, secondly, that the Gaels of Ireland, for more than forty years, were committed almost unanimously to Home Rule.

Other speeches, no doubt, were made,—by Mr. Parnell, Mr. Redmond, and others,—wherein they declared that Home Rule was intended merely as a step towards complete independence; and behind the statue of Parnell in Dublin, is engraved a statement which he made to the effect that he was not one to set bounds to the march of the Irish Nation. Neither, I take it, would any man of sense—to the development of any nation whatever. The most crusted Tory, when swearing allegiance to King George and his heirs for ever, does not mean that in the process of development it can never suit England to take on a republican form of government. Neither does any loyal Canadian or Australian hold that his country, now part of the imperial combination, must remain so always, however its population and resources may develop. They are loyal during the present stage; but they set no bounds to the future development of their country.

And so, I fancy, one can reconcile the speeches of the Irish leaders, by taking them to mean that, whereas, for the present and the near future, Ireland was satisfied to let the Imperial Parliament rule in matters imperial; they—the leaders in question—were not going to bind the Irish people to this for ever, no matter how the population and resources of the country might develop.

10. *Answer to the Question Proposed.*—In view of all this evidence, from both periods of our history,—and much more could easily be added,—I find it hard to allow the claim which Dr. Coffey seems to endorse, to the effect that "England has not now, and never has had, any moral right to rule or govern Ireland"; seeing that "neither the Imperial Parliament since the Union, nor the so-called 'Irish' Parliament before the Union, had ever any moral authority to govern the Irish nation". "An Irishman," he proceeds, "adopting this line of argument",—as Dr. Coffey himself, apparently, does,—"would point out that Ireland was never really conquered, never effectively reduced to complete subjection, till the close of the Williamite wars". But St. Laurence O'Toole, Hugh O'Neill, Hugh Roe O'Donnell, the Confederation of Kilkenny, Owen Roe O'Neill, and the Patriot Parliament of 1689 all had their being before the broken treaty Limerick; and all professed allegiance to kings of England; perhaps because, though their people had not been effectively reduced to complete subjection, those leaders were corrupted by earldoms and such gewgaws. And in the later period, since the Union, when the priesthood of Ireland not only gave up Repeal for Home Rule, but taught their people to regard the English Government as legitimate, under pain of excommunication and eternal death; perhaps they, too, were "detached from loyalty to the interests of their country by place and patronage, by bribery and corruption, and every other form of appeal to selfish interests".[13]

[13] "I. E. Record", *Ibid* p. 489.

Have we not had too much of this corruption charge, levelled against men who, in difficult times, seem to have done their best, according to their lights; which may, no doubt, have deceived them? One would like to know what Dr. Coffey himself,—whose eyes are too widely open to be deceived, as his honour is too bright to allow him to accept place or bribe,—would do, if, when seated in the tribunal of Penance, some poor fellow confessed that he was a member of the Fenian Brotherhood; pleading, as against the decree of the Holy Office, that the English Government in Ireland, against which alone he had plotted, is not legitimate. When we have a public statement on this case, we shall be position to know what Dr. Coffey, and the theologians and canonists who seem to agree with him, really hold as to the binding force of the laws that now emanate from Westminster.

CHAPTER IV

OF THE POSSIBILITY OF LOSS OF
NATIONHOOD WITHOUT ACQUIESCENCE;
AND OF PRESCRIPTION BETWEEN NATIONS

1. *THE Question.*—It is a relief to pass from those comparatively unimportant questions of history to the broad ethical principle that serves as major premiss in Dr. Coffey's argument: that "an unjust conquest . . . can of itself give no moral right to governing authority: in other words that Might is not Right; that the government *de facto* set up by the conquering nation or state, to rule the conquered nation, is not by the mere fact a *de jure* or rightful government; furthermore, that it cannot become so by the mere lapse of time; that, in order to become so, it must at least govern the subject people in such an equitable manner and with such attention to their common good that it will gradually secure the acquiescence—not of the ascendancy party merely, and not, of course, of all the citizens numerically, for this would be impossible,—but of the masses of the people substantially, so that it can be truly described as government with the consent of the governed."

This I have condensed,—I hope, not unfairly,—into the following brief statement:—No fully independent nation ceases to be so *de jure* unless by the free consent of its people. Let us see how the principle works out in practice.

2. *The Milesian Conquest of Ireland.*—According to Professor MacNeill, by far the greater part of Ireland, from the time of St. Patrick to the coming of the Normans, was inhabited by what he calls pre-Milesian peoples, whom the Milesian invaders had reduced to subjection. Ossory, he says, was not subdued; nor the northeast corner of the island, now the counties of Down and Antrim. Everywhere else the pre-Milesians went

down; losing not only political independence but their rights in the soil. They had been independent; as much as were the Milesian conquerors later, till the coming of the Normans. One wonders whether it is Dr. Coffey's view that the pre-Milesian tribes are still *de iure* lords of those lost territories. Or did they freely and formally renounce their rights? Or were they so equitably governed by the Milesians, that they must be held to have acquiesced in their degradation?

In this connection it is well to bear in mind that they are, in the main, the same people who could never be brought to acquiesce in the domination of the English; perhaps because they were treated so much more horribly by these. We know what the men of Leinster thought of the Boru tribute; as well as what any man will think of those who deprived him, or his fathers, of lordship in the land.

3. *Conquest by the Normans.*—When the Normans came, and the Geraldines, for instance, took over so many broad and fertile estates in Leinster and Munster, reducing the Milesian proprietors to the condition of serfs, one wonders whether, in the opinion of Dr. Coffey, the new masters became owners *de iure*; or had they the consent of the mass of the Gael? Could we conceive an Earl of Desmond troubled in conscience over his position, and consulting some professor of ethics of the period, what answer should he receive? If, to make amends for misdeeds and secure rest for his soul, he were to propose to some Bishop to devote part of his estates,—plundered from some Gaelic proprietor,—to the founding of an abbey or the endowment of a church, would it have been the clergyman's duty to decline, as certain Methodists or Baptists in the United States are said to have refused a donation from Mr. J. D. Rockefeller? What, one wonders, would Dr. Coffey have done in the circumstances? What would he do even now? For injustice, it seems, is not righted by lapse of time, however great, without the consent, or acquiescence, of the person who suffered wrong, or his representative. And Dr. Coffey himself gives us to understand how the Gaelic peasants,—formerly Gaelic landowners,—regarded the title of Cromwellian and Williamite spoilers. Perhaps they thought differently of the

Normans; who had despoiled their fathers no less efficaciously or severely.

4. *Conquests by White Men Generally.*—Turning elsewhere, one sees, beyond the ocean,—in America, Africa, Australia, New Zealand; wherever White Men have settled since the time of Columbus—fertile plains, once owned by Red or Black Men, now held by Whites; while the former owners look on sullenly, in degradation. Perhaps they were ousted with greater right than the Gaelic proprietors of Ireland? Or, possibly, the aborigines of North and South America, Africa, Australia, or New Zealand, are so satisfied with the equitable government of their conquerors, as to acquiesce? Not, of course, this or that unreasonable chief or tribesman; but the people as a whole. One would like to have the private opinion, say, of the Red Indians on the matter; or of an assembly of Zulu chiefs.

Perhaps, if Dr. Coffey were made Archbishop of New York, or Boston, or Sydney, he would deem it his duty to hand over to the natural heirs of its former proprietors the real estate of the diocese—churches and presbyteries; diocesan seminary; and so much other ecclesiastical property. Matters like these, no doubt, disturb the slumbers of the Bishops, priests, and religious who now hold this plunder. How crude the doctrine looks when viewed in this way, in the light of what one sees everywhere around!

5. *Teaching of Lessius.*—Let us turn to authority—the great Catholic writers on Justice; among whom Leonard Lessius, the Jesuit, holds a foremost place. He taught at Louvain at the beginning of the seventeenth century; and puts himself a question to our purpose. Needless to say, the tyrant whom he contemplates may be, not an individual, but a usurping State.

"Does a tyrant sin by usurping judgment, and are his decisions void?

"It is to be noted that a tyrant may be so by usurpation of power (such as he who, without any right, has invaded a country and holds it in bondage); while another is so by use of power, being true sovereign otherwise and having legitimate authority. Here we contemplate one who is a tyrant by usurpation and now rules in peace; the country no longer resisting him, for lack of means. For, as regards the true sovereign, it is plain that he does not sin by usurpation of judgment; provided he judges according to the laws, even though he govern tyrannically otherwise.

"Sotus teaches that a tyrant who has invaded a country cannot make any law or pronounce any sentence that binds in conscience; and that, accordingly, his sentences are void. Francis Victoria holds the contrary.

"I reply and say—First: A tyrant of this kind sins by usurpation of judgment, when he gives a decision; though his sentences are valid and the citizens are bound to obey them, till they have been quashed.

"The first point is proved, since, by giving judgment, he usurps the power of the sovereign, and acts as sovereign, which he is not in truth. He sins, therefore, by usurpation of judgment; for whoever usurps the authority of another, and intends to use it in trial, sins by usurpation.

"You will say that he may have sinned, indeed, by invading the sovereignty and usurping that authority; but that he does not sin afterwards, provided he uses it duly, as is expedient for the State; since that is deemed to be the mind of the State. Nay, he would sin if he were to omit giving judgment.

"I reply, by denying the second part of the minor. For he sinned not only by invading the country, but even afterwards he sins continually, as well he as his heirs, by holding it in bondage subject to themselves; until, at length, either he is voluntarily received by the kingdom, (as may happen, if it is independent, and subject to no other sovereign); or, after a long interval of time, prescription is generated".[1]

---

[1] "Utrum tyrannus peccet usurpatione iudicii, eiusque sententiae sint irritae. Notandum est, alium esse tyrannum usurpatione potestatis, (qualis est, qui absque ullo iure Remp. invasit et oppressam tenet); alium usu regiminis, cum alias sit verus Princeps, legitimam potestatem obtinens. Nos hic loquimur de eo qui usurpatione potestatis tyrannus est, et iam in pace imperat; Repub. non amplius ei resistente virium defectu. Nam de vero Principe constat eum non peccare usurpatione iudicii; modo secundum leges iudicet, etiamsi alias tyrannice gubernet.

So far Lessius; who plainly distinguishes two ways in which usurpation which began unjustly may be legitimised: first, by voluntary acceptation of the new régime; and secondly by prescription.

6. *Prescription between Nations.*—I know,—and, in any case, the writer in "The Irish Theological Quarterly" reminds us,—that authority can be quoted for the view that there is no prescription as between nations. But one can find authority for the silliest views; for the view, for instance, that military conscription is never obligatory; or that it is only in virtue of an act of the State one can transfer the dominion of property after death.

To give the "Quarterly" writer his due, he does not seem to attach much weight to these authorities; seeing that he goes on to insist, as a requirement for valid prescription, on "peaceful enjoyment of usurped claims", and "acknowledgment of these by the victims such as never existed in all the troubled years of misrule in Ireland". Even this he proposes merely as a view,

"Sotus (Lib. 3, qu. 4, art. 6) docet tyrannum qui Rempub. invasit non posse ferre ullam legem, nec ius dicere, quod obliget in conscientia; ac proinde sententias eius esse irritas. Contrarium docet Franciscus Victoria (*Relectione de Potestate Civili*, num. 23). Pro solutione

"Respondeo et Dico:—Primo, Tyrannus huiusmodi peccat usurpatione iudicii ius dicendo; sententiae tamen ipsius sunt validae, et tenentur cives illis obtemperare, donec irritentur.

"Prior pars probatur, quia iudicando usurpat sibi potestatem Principis, et gerit se ut verus Princeps, cum revera non sit. Ergo peccat usurpatione iudicii. Qui enim usurpat sibi potestatem alienam, et intendit ea uti in iudicando, peccat usurpatione iudicii.

"Dices, Ille quidem peccavit invadendo principatum et illam auctoritatem sibi usurpando; non tamen peccat postea, si ea debito modo et ut Reipubl. expedit utatur; quia ea censetur esse mens Reipubl. Imo si omitteret ius dicere, peccaret.

"Respondeo negando secundam partem assumpti; quia non solum peccavit Rempubi. invadendo, sed etiam postea assidue peccat, tum ipse tum eius haeres, eam oppressam sibique subiectam servando; donec tandem vel sponte a regno suscipiatur, (quod fiieri potest, si illud sit sai iuris, nulli alteri Principi obnoxium), vel longo temporum intervallo tandem nascatur praescriptio".—*De Iustitia et Iure*, Lib. II. cap. xxix. Dub.ix.]

that might be, and probably is, held by some; not necessarily by himself; who, in the next paragraph adverts to that decree wherein the Holy Office recognises the legitimacy of English rule in Ireland. In view of which and other such "ecclesiastical facts", "a cautious signatory" of the protest against conscription for Ireland may "think it just as wise not to involve himself in these dangerous theories". He will, that is, have sense enough to admit that, whether the Red Indians have or have not acknowledged the claims of the whites to the woods and lakes and prairies of North America,—and there has been less acknowledgment here than in the case of Ireland,—the matter was so definitely settled long ago that it could not be unsettled now without causing such confusion as the law of nature could not allow.

7. *Acquiescence not Necessary.*—If it is silly to maintain that there can be no prescription between nations, it is just as silly to require as a condition of validity an acknowledgment of the usurped claims on the part of the victim nation. No plundered people ever yet made such acknowledgment; except, as just explained, in the sense that, where a social upheaval has settled definitely, so that it cannot be unsettled now without general confusion, it is unreasonable, and therefore wrong, to be the cause of this. The necessity of avoiding such confusion is at the root of all the natural law of justice, and of every right and obligation whatever.

Accordingly, I hold it as a principle of ethics that a nation fully independent at one time may become subject to another, usurping, people, without any consent on the part of those who are subjected. In like manner, I hold that a dynasty, such as that of the Bourbons in France or the Stuarts in England, may lose their right to rule, against their consent; and therefore, of course, without any exercise of the supreme dominion which, till they were deprived of it, was held by them alone in the State.

8. *Time Required.*—Should you ask,—a not unnatural question,—how long it takes to effect such a social upheaval and settlement as I contemplate, my answer would be that no definite limit of time can be determined; any more than for the formation of a species or variety in biology. Such convulsions

are usually of gradual and slow development; but when things have become ripe, the upheaval is catastrophic as a rule. The consequent settlement takes more time; but not so very long. So it was in France at the time of the great Revolution; and so also has the upheaval taken place in Russia and Germany. Let us hope that in these countries also the settlement will not be long delayed.

CHAPTER V

OF THREE DEGREES OF CONQUEST; AND OF THE EFFICACY OF FORCED CONSENT TO TRANSFER OF AUTHORITY.

1. *INDIRECT Authority of Usurper.*—Lessius, continuing the disquisition already quoted, shows how the decrees of a usurping power may be valid, even before it has been legitimised by consent or prescription; and how, even when it is not yet legitimate, the conquered people may be bound to submit:— "The usurper's sentences and just commands, though deriving no force from his own authority, have it otherwise. First, and inchoately, from the natural law, which, supposing that state of things, dictates obedience, for the public weal. Otherwise everything would be full of theft and robbery. Secondly, and fully, from the country; and this either because, while such condition lasts, it [the country] gives him authority by some kind of tacit consent; since it wishes him to administer justice and duly perform the duties of the office which he has usurped; or, rather, since it tacitly approves whatever acts and commands of his are in conformity with the laws and with common utility; and it wants just sentences,whereby the disputes of the citizens are settled and the guilty are punished,—to be valid, and the subjects to be bound. For unless they were valid and obligatory, no one would obey, except in seeming; but in secret everyone would do the opposite, to the great inconvenience of the State. But the State can give this force to the sentences and acts of an usurper; since, though oppressed by tyranny, it is the superior of everyone, and can regard the sentences of the usurper as its own"[1].

[1] "Eius sententiae et iusta mandata, etsi non habeant vim a tyrannica potestate, habent tamen aliunde; primo et inchoative a iure naturali,

In like manner Dr. Coffey writes[2]:—"when a nation is thus tyrannically held in subjection by the superior force of a dominant State, and thus unjustly deprived of its own rightful government, its people are morally bound by the natural law to obey the measures imposed upon them by the usurper; not, indeed, because these measures have themselves the moral force of laws (for they have not), but because and in so far as obedience to these measures is the only means of procuring and safeguarding certain goods which every social community is morally bound to secure, namely, public peace and order, and its own preservation from total extinction through the bootless sacrifice of the lives of its citizens,—a sacrifice which would be the inevitable result of a sustained trial of strength with the usurper".

This principle Dr. Coffey applies to the condition of Ireland since the Union; that is, on the supposition,—which he seems to endorse,—that laws made by the Imperial Parliament have not of themselves any force to bind the Irish people, for lack of consent on their part. I do not think it unfair to suppose that he would apply the principle no less to the condition of Ireland before the Union, from the time of the Norman conquest; which, as an unjust usurpation, in which the Irish nation never acquiesced, gave no legislative authority. So I understand his argument.

quod, supposito tali rerum statu, dictat esse obtemperandum, propter bonum commune; alioquin omnia essent plena furtis et latriciniis. Secundo et complete a Republ.; idque vel quia, durante illo statu, tacito quodam consensu, dat ei auctoritatem, dum vult ut ille iustitiam administret, et officio usurpato debito modo fungatur; vel potius quia tacite approbat eius mandata et acta, legibus et utilitati communi consentanea, et vult sententias iustas, quibus lites civium dirimuntur, et sontes plectuntur, esse validas et subditos obligari. Nisi enim validae essent et obligarent, nemo nisi in specie obtemperaret; sed quisque occulte faceret contrarium, cum magno Reipubl. incommodo. Potest autem hanc vim sententiis et actis tyranni dare, quia est singuloroum superior, etiamsi tyrannice sit oppressa, et iustas tyranni sententias pro suis habere". *Ibid.* n. 73.

[2] "Irish E. Record", *Ibid.* p. 488.

To the abstract principle I have no objection; though I have my doubts as to whether it can be applied to the case of Ireland, whether before or after the Union; and this apart from the evidence, set forth already, of consent to English rule on the part of our people. Suppose there was no free consent, but unjust usurpation by England, the question arises whether laws made for Ireland by the usurper would be of themselves invalid, as being based on pressure unjustly exercised to secure the adhesion of the conquered people.

2. *Three Degrees of Conquest.*—In this connection, I think we can distinguish three degrees of conquest; and I will ask you to allow me to illustrate what I mean from the relations of France and Belgium to Germany; which, though not quite parallel with those of England and Ireland, are sufficiently like for our purpose; besides having the great advantage of allowing us a more dispassionate view.

In the conquest of France, or of part of that country, by Germany, I distinguish three grades of completeness: first, that of Champagne, during the last four years of war; second, that of Alsace, since the war of 1870; and third, acquisition of territory further east, on the left bank of the Rhine, which we may suppose Gaelic tribes to have held at one time.

Supposing, now, that not only the late war but that of 1870 were unjust on the part of Germany; and also that she acted unjustly when, in the remote past, she colonised the left bank of the Rhine; her rule, though deriving from usurpation in each of the three districts, would not be of the same character and authority in each. She would have had no jurisdiction in Champagne; wherein the people would be only indirectly bound to her decrees, as explained by Dr. Coffey. She would have had true, though revocable, jurisdiction in Alsace. And in the land bordering the Rhine, where she had long been settled, her jurisdiction would be irrevocable; except in so far as the authority of any State in any of its provinces is revocable, in accordance with the laws of development.

Take, first, the difference between Champagne and Alsace. This latter province was ceded formally by the Treaty of Frankfurt; whereas the French people fought to the last for

Champagne. Did this make no ethical difference? And was the Treaty of Frankfurt devoid of any force whatever, even on the supposition that its signature was due to unjust pressure on the part of Germany?

3. *Effect of Forced Acquiescence.*—Every handbook on Moral Theology gives what is now, practically, recognised in the Catholic schools as the effect of forced consent to a contract. There was, indeed, some difference of opinion at one time; a few holding that where, as in the case before us, the pressure is supposed to be unjust, any resulting contract is quite invalid. Against this, the great body of our moralists,—whose opinion St. Alphonsus calls[3] "most probable and most common",—regard it as valid; while, of those who hold this view, almost all agree that such a contract may be rescinded at the will of the aggrieved party, whenever he can conveniently do so. He can, moreover, rescind of his own immediate right, without any overriding judicial sentence.

According to this, the act whereby France ceded Alsace at the Peace of Frankfurt, was valid, and gave Germany true jurisdiction over the territory ceded; even though we suppose the treaty to have been signed by the French plenipotentiaries under the influence of undue pressure; provided always they gave true consent—which is to be presumed. This does not imply that France may not now be within her right in denouncing the treaty in that part, and recalling her act of cession; a question which does not concern us now.

As regards Champagne, on the contrary, there was no cession, whether spontaneous or due to pressure; so that the German occupation, if unjust, would not give true jurisdiction, but would merely base a duty of indirect compliance, as already set forth. With regard to the Rhine provinces, German authority,—though, possibly, deriving originally from usurpation,—would have been made valid by prescription; apart altogether from any consent on the part of the ousted Gaels.

It has often happened that a national dispute terminated without formal treaty, when the conquered people were beaten

---

[3] *Theol. Moral.*, L. iii., n. 716.

so as to be incapable of further struggle. When this happens, they consent to the transfer of dominion; under pressure, no doubt, which very often is unjust; but they consent really, till they are in position to resume the fight. It is, of course, conceivable that they should yield without recognising any dominion on the part of the conqueror; as when an individual delivers his purse to a robber. But when the cession takes place by way of formal treaty, it is more reasonable, I think, to presume that the consent is real; and the same applies, I fancy, when the cession is informal. Any way, there either is or is not consent to the transfer. Where there is no consent, and the conquest has been effected by unjust use of force, dominion does not pass; at least until the new order has become so stable as to found a title in prescription. When consent has been extorted,— real consent, extorted by unjust pressure,—dominion passes; and equitable laws made by the new authorities are valid in themselves, till the act of cession has been effectually recalled.

4. *Ireland not like Belgium.*—One often hears Ireland under English rule compared to Belgium under the rule of the Germans; as if there were not this great difference, that, whereas the King of the Belgians with his government, representing the nation, never ceased to fight; and so, in the most effectual manner, to record the national dissent from the transfer of dominion which Germany attempted; we in Ireland gave up the struggle. I have given evidence to show that in pre-Union times we formally recognised, more than once, the dominion of the King of England; and that since the Union we recognised the jurisdiction of the Imperial Parliament.

Even supposing all this due to unjust pressure, still the consent was there; revocable, no doubt, on the supposition; but giving the alien ruler true dominion till it was effectually recalled.

Possibly it was recalled during the Repeal agitation, through the influence of O'Connell; but is it not conceivable that O'Connell may have consented to the rule of the Imperial Parliament even while agitating for Repeal; striving to get that body to relinquish its authority; but recognising the authority till relinquished. From the fact that he sat in Parliament, and took the oath of allegiance, I have argued that this was his real mind.

In any case, consent was renewed once more under the
Home Rule leaders. Has it been since recalled, in the Sinn
Féin movement; wherein not much more than one-third of the
electors voted for an independent Republic; while it is well
known that, of those who voted that way, a considerable
number did so merely to oust the old Parliamentary Party or
to secure a fuller measure of Home Rule?

These are matters of fact, as to which I have no special
competence. The ethical principle, with which I am concerned,
is, that usurpation, even when unjust, may give a valid title to
jurisdiction, apart even from prescription; and that it does
give it whenever the nation despoiled really consents to the
cession of its rights.

CHAPTER VI

OF THE EFFECT OF A TRANSFER OF JURISDICTION SECURED BY CORRUPTION

1. *LACK of Theological Authority.*—One of the most serious and apparently well-founded charges against the Imperial Parliament, is that its title to rule Ireland is based on the Act of Union; and that, as this was passed through flagrant corruption, it does not embody the consent of the Irish people. Let us examine this as dispassionately as we can.

There is, I regret to say, little scientific authority to guide us, despite all that Catholic moralists have written on almost every aspect of injustice. They dispute, at great length, whether one who has taken money for doing what should not be done, may keep the money after doing his wicked part. The question before us, however, is, not whether the venal members of the Irish Parliament could retain their bribes; but whether their purchased votes were valid, in the sense of availing to make the Act of Union binding on the Irish people.

2. *Analogies.*—It is a question which I have often heard discussed under other aspects—as regards the votes of other representatives city aldermen, for instance, and county or district councillors; who, though they might feel insulted by an offer of money for a vote, are not above recording it to secure offices for their friends, or even bargaining for an equivalent on the next occasion. About the ethical value of transactions of this kind I have heard some discussions, on the part of moralists of keen intelligence, wide reading, and long experience; who, nevertheless, did not seem to have arrived at any definite conclusion; whereas every budding orator or pressman can decide off-hand that the Act of Union has no ethical value, as being due to corruption.

It is not, however, orators or politicians merely who have instructed us in this way, but statesmen of the rank and experience of Mr. Gladstone; who, you would fancy, never offered any man a consideration for a vote. He did not, of course, offer so much down; but neither, as far as I know, did Pitt or Castlereagh. They gave titles, places, compensation for vested interests, money for press work. But did Mr. Gladstone never give a title for party services; or a pension; or some valuable consideration to the press? Did he never stave off opposition to some measure by an offer of a seat in the cabinet, or a place in the government, or of compensation for some interest that he was about to extinguish? Have we not even heard of titles being given for donations to the funds of both the great English Parties? Let us try to give even Castlereagh the measure of justice we mete out to others, and which, possibly, we may ourselves require.

3. *Election of Unworthy Clergymen to Ecclesiastical Benefices.*— In the absence of authoritative guidance we can only go by analogy, in so far as this is available; and I find that Father Lehmkuhl, S.J.,—a well-known and respected authority in the modern Catholic schools of Morals,—when discussing the effect of collation of an ecclesiastical benefice on some unworthy clergyman, teaches that the act is valid, however unfit the recipient may be; unless it should be a case wherein the canons interfere to quash the election. Otherwise the election is valid, though liable to be quashed.[1]

Here we have an exercise of authority deriving from others: for it is not by any power of his own that an elector may appoint to a benefice. He is supposed to transgress his mandate,—if, indeed, it be a mandate,—by electing some one who is unworthy. And yet the act is valid.

It would, no doubt, be quashed *ipso facto* in case of an ecclesiastical appointment, if secured by simony. That, however, is special legislation due to the reverence of the Church for sacred things. If the position were, for instance, that of medical officer to a dispensary district, which some one secured

[1] *Theol. Moral.* i. n. 1159; note 2. iii.

by bribing one or more of the electors, as far as I know, the appointment would be valid; though, I suppose, it would be quashed if the corruption were proved in court.

4. Ethics of Agency.—As far as I can discern the intrinsic reasons on which Father Lehmkuhl's teaching is based, they are connected with the ethics of agency; the supposition being that those who are empowered to appoint to ecclesiastical benefices do not act in their own name. So also, I take it, members of parliament and other such bodies do not act in their own name, but as agents; if not of those who elected them, then of the country or district. They seem, moreover, to have received a general, rather than a special mandate; being commissioned, not for this or that individual act or purpose, but, in the case of members of parliament, to transact the affairs of the country generally. County and district councillors, similarly, have a mandate to transact the affairs of the county or district which is administered by the body to which they belong.

Now, one who has received a general mandate does not act invalidly whenever his action is opposed to the interest of his principal. Such action, I admit, is unjust,—lacks, that is, distributive justice, at least,—but, if it were invalid, no soft bargain made by such an agent would bind in conscience; for the simple reason that, being soft, it was not in the interest of those by whom the agent was commissioned. One cannot, however, go so far as that.

Even, therefore, though parliament should make a bargain which is not to the advantage of the nation, the act is valid, provided it comes within the commission which parliament received. And even though of the majority by whom the act was passed some acted from corrupt motives,—having taken a place, or compensation, or even a downright bribe,—this would not of itself invalidate the act; as it would not invalidate a sale—of cattle, let us say—if an agent who had been duly commissioned to sell them, did so for less than the medium price, pocketing a tip for his complaisance to the purchaser. He could and should be punished for such conduct; which I regard as being not only immoral but strictly unjust—to his principal. A law, moreover, that might empower a court to quash such contracts, I should consider just. But, till the contract has been duly quashed in that way, I should deem valid.

It is, I admit, a difficult question, as to which we are sadly in need of expert guidance. But if that is enough to make a prudent moralist hesitate, would it not be well to hesitate before delivering an adverse judgment on the validity of an act of parliament such as that of the Legislative Union of Great Britain and Ireland; especially should the decision be embodied in a dissertation that may be supposed to deal with the question with expert authority?

5. *Commission of Grattan's Parliament.*—Dr. Coffey, I know, is disposed to endorse the plea of those who deny the commission of Grattan's Parliament—that it was elected by the Irish People or could speak or act for them. Here, again, we have to seek a principle; and I cannot help entertaining doubts as to that on which this plea, of lack of commission, is based.

There is no denying that Grattan's Parliament was in need of reform: the franchise was too restricted and the seats divided inequitably. The same, however, could be said of the English Parliament of the period—that it needed reform, as regards both the extension of the franchise and distribution of seats. Should we, then, hold that acts of the English Parliament were not valid, for lack of due commission, towards the close of the eighteenth century ?

Where, moreover, will you find a parliament that is not in need of reform? It was only the other day that English women got the franchise; as, I suppose, is their due. Suffragists, at least, think so. Does it follow that, because we now regard them as having a right to vote, acts of parliament which were passed before they could vote have no binding force? Or, as some women have not yet got votes who may get them in a year or two, is it possible that all the work of the present Parliament is so much waste energy?

So it may be with regard to the method of voting; which probably, should secure proportional representation. Or it may be that young men of eighteen, who are liable for military service, are entitled to vote for members of parliament and of local councils. And, no doubt, reforms will yet be made in the proportion in which seats in these bodies are distributed. Are we to regard it as a principle of ethics that, till the whole is settled equitably, so as to leave no room for further reform, the acts of such assemblies will have no binding force ?

Consider one of the consequences. The Bolshevists of Russia, I understand, repudiate the loans accepted by that country under the government of the Tsars; on the ground that the nation gave no commission to those who contracted those obligations. Does that plea hold in justice? And may Great Britain, similarly, and other nations repudiate their debts, on the ground that the parliaments which contracted them had no commission from the women, who in every nation form the majority?

6. *Principle Suggested.*—Can it be that, for validity, all that is needed is observance of the constitution for the time in being? That if the king alone is empowered by the constitution to make laws, as in early feudal times, then he can make them of his own authority, without consulting parliament? As also that, if he is required to act through parliament, the assembly through which he must act is just what the constitution determines for the time? This, indeed, might lack some kind of justice, and need reform; but, however inequitable, its acts would be valid all the same.

I do not presume to say that this is the true principle that governs the question; but I do say that there is at least as much to be said for it as there is for any which I can find underlying this plea of invalidity of the Act of Union, for lack of commission on the part of the assembly by which it was passed.

It is another question whether such an act, though valid, may not demand reconsideration and reform. This also I should answer in the affirmative.

CHAPTER VII

OF HOW A PEOPLE HITHERTO INDEPENDENT MAY BE BOUND TO UNION WITH OTHERS; AND OF HOW THIS MAY BE SECURED

1. *APPLICATION of the Principle of Development.*—I have been assuming hitherto that whatever consent the Irish people gave to the present mode of governing their country, was extorted by force, and that this pressure was unjust on the part of England. The latter part of the assumption is not admitted by English statesmen; and it is well to consider their point of view. It will be found to be bound up with the doctrine of development; which, in one form or other, has revolutionised history and science. The English view, as I understand it, is that in the British Islands, as elsewhere in Europe,—Germany and Italy, for instance,—a time came when kingdoms and principalities hitherto independent were bound to unite in self-defence; and that, when this became due, no injustice could be done in pressing to secure the necessary union.

2. *Self-Determination and Self-Defence.*—This, we hear, is the day of small nationalities when the civilised world allows each of them to determine for itself how it will be governed: in absolute independence or as part of a united kingdom, empire, or republic. Whereupon the question arises, Whether this right of self-determination is an ethical principle; and, if so, how far does it extend? Have the German States, for instance, or those of Italy, a right to separate government? One knows what Bismarck would say, or Cavour; but perhaps they were despots.

We find historically, as far as I know, that what we call the nations of Europe are all combinations of what were once independent states which, in their condition of separation, lived in antagonism, often intensified into warfare; as may be illustrated from the annals of our own country. Greece went down, because, for all her culture, she could not combine her warring petty states; while Rome succeeded for the opposite reason, though she had to take her science and art from Greece.

Nearer home, Britain, when the Roman armies left, was as weak as Ireland, if not weaker; but the British seem to have had the Roman sense for combination: hence their success. First, the Kingdom of England was formed, from the Heptarchy; then Wales came in, and Scotland; these three previously warring states combining to form the nucleus of what has long been the wealthiest and most powerful empire in the world.

Is it an ethical principle that the petty kingdoms of the Heptarchy might, without doing wrong, have remained isolated to the present? Or that Scotland and Wales were no less free to refuse combination? This I find it hard to believe.

3. *Pre-Milesian States of Ireland: The United States.*—We hear, moreover, a good deal of the Irish Nation, one and indivisible; and how Ulster should submit to the rule of the majority. But what of that corner of Ulster, now called Down and Antrim, which, Professor MacNeill assures us, was never subdued by the Milesians? And what of Ossory, that other Pre-Milesian state, which, according to the same authority, "retained its independent and native rulers till the time of the English confiscation under Queen Mary, and even later, and was the longest established Celtic principality in the world"? Were these free to remain in their isolation? And are they now free to resume, if ever they renounced it freely? If not, in what sense is the right of self-determination an ethical principle?

Those who know the United States tell us that South differs very much from North; and East from Middle-West and West; not, indeed, in language; religion, or possibly in race; but in mentality, customs, financial interests and conditions. The differences came to a head, as North and South, at the time of the Civil War, when the southern states wanted to break away from the Union—asserting their right to self-determination, and that no one should govern them without their consent. Lincoln did not admit it, nor the North; and the world, I fancy, now holds that Lincoln was right. How, then, of self-determination and government only by consent of the governed?

4. *Principle of Combination.*—In view of which, and of ever so much more that might be gathered from the history of every nation in the world, I beg to submit the following as an ethical principle, roughly outlined, and possibly needing amendment:— A time may come in the development of peoples, when their interest requires them to combine, for advance and protection; and when this happens they do wrong to maintain separate independence.

It is, in my opinion, the mistake, amounting to crime, committed not only by the Red Indian and other uncultured tribes, but by the Irish clans, and by the ancient Greeks, the most cultured people known to history. It was a sin against patriotism; which, wherever committed, called down its own punishment.

5. *Union May be Secured by Pressure.*—This introduces a further principle, already set forth in *Some Aspects of the Social Question,* to the effect that; When an individual, tribe, or nation, attempts what is inequitable in any way, it is not wrong for another whose equitable rights are thereby violated to use reasonable force to protect itself. And, further still, Though it is not permissible to have recourse to fraud, in any case, or to bribery; no injury is done to any individual or nation that may be restrained thereby from doing what is unjust or inequitable.

I do not know how Bismarck contrived to make a united Germany; but should not be surprised if he had to have recourse to threats, or even to fraud. The man who precipitated a great war by deliberate falsification of a state paper, was not above either, to carry a measure on which he had set his heart. Nor would any patriotic German now blame him for having used reasonable pressure to make Bavaria, for instance, enter the Bund, under a Prussian Kaiser; nor, if fraud were used, would it be deemed worse than fraud: certainly not injustice to Bavaria. Lincoln, similarly, did not hesitate to wage a great war to prevent the southern states from consummating the crime of separation from the Union; nor does any moderate man blame him for such use of force.[1]

The pity was that in Ireland, as in Greece, no one was found strong enough to consolidate the different states. Brian Boru, they say, nearly succeeded with the Irish; and had he succeeded, even by crushing the Ossory and Leinster men, he would have made himself a name as a great and beneficent patriot, more illustrious and enduring than he has drawn from the battle of Clontarf. Few Ossory men would now deny that their fathers were wrong in asserting the right of self-determination against him.

6. *Application to Modern Ireland.*—Passing on to the application of these principles, I think it will be seen that, whereas the English, like the early Romans, were and are modest enough to admit that without union they could not have the security or prosperity they desired; we in Ireland, like the ancient Greek states, have been and are self-confident—that we are sufficient of ourselves. England admits, nay pleads, that she needs to have Scotland, Wales, and Ireland closely united with her, in one imperial, military and fiscal system; as Germany is united. Scotland admits the need; as does Wales; though both have shown that they could live alone at least as well as we; while they were once as bitterly opposed to England as ever we were. They have had the good sense to control their spleen, in the interest of national welfare. The north-east of Ireland wants the Union—those great business interests that centre in Belfast. So do the business men of Ireland everywhere.

The benefit deriving from this imperial union to all the components I take to have been the motive that attracted Pitt, as also Castlereagh. It was certainly Gladstone's idea; as it is that of Mr. Lloyd George and Mr. Asquith; all of whom,

---

[1] In the newspapers of April 14, 1919, there appeared an official *communiqué* giving a summary of the Covenant of the League of Nations. The following clause is to our present purpose: "States not members of the League will be invited to accept the obligations of the League for the purpose of particular disputes; and, if they fail to comply, maybe coerced."

no doubt, looked primarily to the interest of Great Britain, but may well have been under the honest impression that both islands would benefit by the union. To compass this some of them did shady things; but those who recognise the Union as being anything like the good these statesmen deemed it, have little blame for the tricks to which they had recourse. We have seen that Germans do not think much the less of Bismarck for any guile he may have used to entice Bavaria into the Imperial Bund; nor even for using pressure to that purpose; as I should not blame Pitt very much if I could persuade myself that the Union was to the advantage of Ireland as well as of Great Britain.

That was, is, and will be, the real question between the two countries: is the Union for the good of both? and, if so, under what conditions? There can be little doubt that England benefits; and would benefit still more if we in Ireland were to fall in heartily. The question, then, reduces itself to this: whether and under what conditions union with England is for the interest of the Irish people.

It is not, primarily, a question of ethics; but of business, or of politics; and therefore outside the sphere on which I can speak with any competence. But as it has been discussed by so many, with no very extraordinary claims to business capacity, perhaps I may be allowed to put in a word.

7. *Irish Trade Dependent on That of Britain.*—For more than half a century now I have been watching Irish trade; not, of course, with anything like the attention that is given by men of business. And I have noticed, first, that we have little commerce except with England; and, secondly, that what trade we have is sympathetic with hers; sharing, almost immediately, with its least buoyancy or depression.

Thus while England confesses that she wants our help in trade, we, who pretend we have no great need of her, sink or swim with her in spite of ourselves. We are united with her in bonds closer even than the Act of Union—those of trade; and if it is her interest to be prosperous, it is ours to see her prosper. Contributing to her prosperity, we secure our own. Had she failed in the late war, and been bled white, we should have been beggared; so that those of us who fought for her, whether with silver or leaden bullets, fought for our own country; and those who wished success to Germany, wished, however unwittingly, impoverishment to Ireland.

8. *Who Saved our Trade?*—When I put this argument, as I often have, to friends who think differently, they gave me one of two answers—sometimes both. First, that, even though we took no part in the war, England would continue rich and prosperous, and our trade with her would remain. Secondly, that, even though she failed and were reduced to poverty, our trade would remain; no longer, indeed, trade with her, but with whatever country might benefit by her impoverishment. May I be allowed to say what I think of all this?

First, England has come through the war; with a pile of debt, and, so far, impoverished but not bled white, as she would have been, had she lost. Her commerce, which is the basis of ours, remains, as we hope. The common interest has been safeguarded: through whose efforts? Not by ours, who drew off in the time of greatest need. During the Irish land-war there were farmers who took no part in the struggle, but were among the first to secure whatever profit could be drawn from the victory. Among the working classes there are always some who join no union, and who retain their jobs and pay, while the union men, out on strike, suffer cold and hunger. Those non-unionists and non-strikers benefit for the occasion; as do all scabs and black-legs; but theirs, in the end, is the sure way to slavery.

It was so the Irish clans went down in the struggle with the Normans; some looking on and gloating over the discomfiture of old enemies, their kinsmen, whose comrades in arms they ought to have been. England has come through; and so far our commerce has been saved; but it was done at a tremendous sacrifice of blood and treasure; while so many of us looked on with eyes hungry to see the tide of battle set the other way. Was it an honourable way to save our trade?

Secondly, had England failed and lost her commerce, our trade, it is said, would still survive; perhaps even be in a better position. It is a question of business; as to which, though having an opinion of my own, I took occasion, now and then, to question business men. Are you prepared, I asked them, to seek new trade, with Germany, or whatever country may need our produce, should the English market fail? And I did not meet one man of business who liked the prospect. They would have to face it, of course, if the condition were fulfilled; just as they would have to face the Court of Bankruptcy or the workhouse in so many other contingencies. Young priests would face the consequences with light hearts; and university students; those, generally, who either had no business or no business outlook; like so many of our labourers, farmers, and small shop-keepers. But of men of business, not one.

For years before the war we used to hear farmers complain of how hard it was to live, with the ruinous prices due to competition. Well, as far as one can judge, the competition will continue, and become intensified; so that unless those farmers find a market in which they will enjoy special favour, one does not see how they can escape being ruined. Fortunately for them, England has been frightened, by the submarine, into a disposition to show the special favour they need so much. And yet the farmers of Ireland protest that they can stand alone, without British trade favour. It may be magnificent; but it does not look like business.

9. *Other Small Nations.*—I have been reminded, in this con-nection, of the small nations of Europe,—Holland, Belgium, Switzerland, and the Scandinavian countries; how prosperous they were in their isolation; and how foolish it was of Belgium and Roumania to take sides in the war. It is an argument one often heard in the days of the Land League; as one still does in Labour disputes: how sensible those were who did not expose themselves to eviction or loss of wages; or, still more, if they took a farm or a job which some Land Leaguer or striker had resigned. So, too, in the struggle between the Normans and the Irish, clans would remain aloof, hugging themselves on their astuteness, and blind to the fact that the day of trial was coming for themselves.

One does not like to be too hard on Holland and the Scandinavian peoples; who could have been invaded and destroyed by Germany. Seeing what had become of Belgium, one could excuse them; as one could excuse a farmer, during the Land League times, for not facing eviction. It was not heroic; but all cannot be heroes, any more than they can be six foot high. In Ireland we had not even that poor excuse.

Holland, Belgium, Denmark, and Switzerland, would very soon be annexed by Germany, politically or at least economically, did not England, France, Italy, and Russia forbid. Could we in Ireland bring the United States as near as the Low Countries are to France and England, or as Cuba is to Florida, our trade would not be so wholly bound up with that of England, and we should not be in need, as at present, of union with her.

10. *Utilitarianism.*—These, I know, are gross considerations, which abstract from spiritual interests,—what so many call the "soul of the nation"; as if the mother's soul were free from the duty of providing bread-and-butter for her offspring. It is this provision which I think imperilled; not any special Celtic culture,—religion, language, or traditions,—which, under a Home Rule government, in union with England, can take good care of themselves. That is, if we have one-tenth of the grit that is needed to make us prosperous as a fully independent people.

CHAPTER VIII

OF SOME CONDITIONS OF
COMPLETE SELF-DETERMINATION

1. *THE Principle of Self-Determination.*—It is conceivable that even though Ireland, as a whole, was never a united and fully independent nation, she may be such now *de iure,* through development; whereupon it might be argued that a people *de iure* independent are not bound by a law such as that of Conscription passed without their consent. This raises another question: whether the principle of Union, set forth in the last Chapter, may not be pushed too far, so as to run counter to another law, of Self-Determination, as is now the catch-word. Let us, then, consider what Self-Determination means and whether it may not be conditioned.

The principle, as a rule, is worded, rhetorically, in universal terms: Nations—meaning thereby, apparently, people of the same race, language, and mode of culture, who live within definite geographical boundaries,—are entitled to govern themselves. In another form the principle runs thus: No government is legitimate without consent of the governed.

2. *The Principle Conditioned.*—On one occasion I asked a New Zealand soldier,—who had been brought up in Ireland and professed Socialism,—whether the Maoris of his adopted country had this right of self-government; and when I went on to say that it might be found to imply re-occupation of their ancient dominions, my Socialist interlocutor said that they were uncivilised. I have put the same question, and received the same answer, with regard to other undeveloped races: Indians of America, Negroes of South Africa, Bushmen of Australia. These people,—of such distinctive race, language,

culture,—often live within definite geographical boundaries; but, apparently, have no right to Self-Determination, and are governed legitimately without their consent.

I doubt whether any educated—or even any thinking-man, in Ireland or elsewhere, regards the principle of Self-Determination as applying universally: to all peoples which-soever. It is conditioned, by Development; and, so conditioned, is admitted by the most ardent Unionists. The only difference of opinion I perceive is with regard to the Development: whether this or that grade entitles to Self-Determination; and, if so, to how much. For Self-Determination has its degrees.

3. *Development.*—I do not know of any class in England so reactionary as to maintain that all the revolutions that took place in that country were unjustified; and that, by right, England should be ruled to-day as she was before King John was forced by Bishops and Barons to sign the Charter. You will find plenty to complain of the last extension of the franchise; as also of the pressure that was brought to bear on the House of Lords, some years ago, to get that Estate to resign certain rights it had held till then. These are the Tories; but would such typical Conservatives as Mr. A. Balfour or Lord Hugh Cecil leave the people of England as little power of selection of their rulers as they had under the Tudor kings? All states-men are Liberals now, in the sense of admitting the broadening of rights due to national development.

I find it hard to believe there can be a politician or thinker of any class, in Britain, who would claim that *de iure* New England should still be ruled from Westminster; or that, how-ever South Africa or Australia may grow, in resources and population, they will never be entitled to full independence. If, therefore, Development, here and there, results in need of Union; it results as surely, elsewhere, in need of fission; and where this need is, there also will be the right.

In the United States of America no statesman or politician would allow Self-Determination, in the sense of complete independence, to the Philippines—till they have been more fully developed; and as for government by Consent of the governed, we know how Lincoln and the North interpreted that when the Southern states wanted to secede from the Union. Even now, should Venezuela or Colombia think they would do better if united, let us say, with England, as Canada is, one would like to know whether the Government at Washington would allow them that right of Self-Determination.

4. *Principle running through all Forms of Life.*—It is not among nations only the law of Self-Determination holds, but in every form of life; wherein also we may see how it is conditioned. Everyone knows how strawberry-plants send out runners, with a tendency to develop roots at certain nodes; whereby, when these rootlets strike in a suitable place, new plants are formed. These, like colonies, draw sustenance, for a time, from the parent, through the runner; till their own roots have well struck; when they rely more and more on these; the connection with the parent organism becoming gradually useless and disappearing at length. Sever it before the time when the new roots have struck, and what might have been a fruitful plant will wither.

So, too, should bees swarm before the colony that leaves is strong enough to shift for itself; or at a time wherein shifts are vain which in other circumstances might have set it up, the colony will fail unless united with another stock. For such a colony, in such circumstances, the Self-Determination of complete independence is fatal.

And so of men. One does not advise every immature or untrained lad to set up for himself; and even when a young man is entitled to marry and set up a home, he may not be in position to open a business. For this one needs not merely strength of body and culture of mind, but opportunity; for lack of which the best will fail, while others, with lower powers, succeed elsewhere. No one preaches Self-Determination, in the sense of complete independence, to all the clerks and assistants in our business houses. They must qualify for the position of master; and even then they need capital; while the capital that would suffice at one time or place, will be useless at another.

5. *Independence and Competition.*—It is noticeable, moreover, that, as social relations grow complex,—with more rapid communications and freer intercourse,—it becomes more and

more difficult to hold one's place in business. Hence all those combinations, of employers and employed, growing ever wider and wider; all miners forming one great union; and, even so, not being able to hold their own without joining forces with railway-men and transport workers. Labour leaders cry out that it is only by a national union of all working-men these can secure their rights; while international Socialism, at Berne, Stockholm, or elsewhere, insists that merely national unions are useless. No one preaches Self-Determination, in the sense of complete independence and separation, to Labour.

So, too, of Capital. In simpler times, before things were standardised and turned out in heaps, a carpenter, smith, tailor, or bootmaker, could stand alone; but now, even though he may have succeeded in establishing a little factory, he has to combine with some bigger and stronger concern, or else go out. Hence the many amalgamations we see—of railways, shipping companies, steel-works, tobacco factories, soap factories, and what not. Hence combinations of employers, to match and meet those of rival employers, as well as of the working-men.

Even the greatest nations are no longer fully independent, but form leagues; to which, when formed, they must submit. A League that would leave its members fully independent would be worthless. France had to call in England, Italy, America, even Japan, to help her, the other day; and England and the United States had to allow their armies to be commanded by a Frenchman. Full Self-Determination would have lost the war.

It seems, therefore, to be a law of life that Self-Determination is conditioned, by development and environment; so that (1) any organism,—whether vegetable or animal, individual or social,—that sets up for itself prematurely, assuming more independence than its development, in its condition of environment, allows, is sure to fail and will have to pay the penalty; while (2) the same holds of those which continue the struggle in isolation, after the time when, owing to change of environment, they are no longer in position to maintain themselves without combining with others.

6. *Need of Combination Relative.*—This law of combination seems to me far more imperative than is any principle of Self-Determination permissive. It must, however, be borne well in mind that the need of combination is relative: depending on environment, and growing with the competition whereby every living thing is surrounded and pressed; which competition itself increases with increasing facilities of communication. The independence that served the states of ancient Greece left them later an easy prey to Roman power. From the fact that a number of independent Irish clans were so easily vanquished by the Normans, it follows that the independent clan-system was then ruinous; but it does not follow that it had been so always, before the Irish had to face that powerful combination. International regulation of the price of labour is more necessary now than it was before the railway and the steamship had made commerce so international; and whereas a Balance of Power or Holy Alliance might have been fairly sufficient once to keep the peace in Europe, this now requires a League of Nations. As the forces of evil, or of opposition, combine against one, the need increases, for combination with forces of an opposite kind, to maintain one's position.

The Land League movement showed this; as does the Labour movement, and the ever-growing combinations of Capital. Irish farmers who stood aloof from the League, were saved by the very combination they refused to join; as non-union labourers are saved by the unions. Taken singly, any number of rods are easily broken; and *Divide et Impera* is just as true in its way as *Sinn Féin*.

7. *War of Competition but Commencing.*—There are people who hope that we have seen the last of wars; and that in the era of peace, now dawning, as there will be no standing armies or guns, while equal justice reigns everywhere, the weakest and least developed people can get on: that in the new environment they are sure of fair play, if not from this or that grasping neighbour, then from the League. So that in the new world development would not be required as a condition of full nationhood; nor need environment or, competition be reckoned with; but only race, and race-culture—history, mentality, religion and the rest.

Then, perhaps, our old Iverk kingdom,—one of the most ancient in Europe,—will revive; or Ossory, at least, be fully independent; and over the rest of Ireland we can go back to the clan system, with its shadowy High King. Scotland, too, and Wales will separate from England; and England return to a Heptarchy; France, Germany, and Italy split up like Russia; and each of the United States of America set up for itself. What fools men are sure to be!

Even though we had seen the last of wars with shells and bombs, we have scarce come to the beginning of the war of competition which these Saturnian realms are to witness. For it has been left to the ingenuity of these later ages to discover that men can be enslaved as effectually by commerce as by iron chains. Will President Wilson give us any guarantee of freedom from this kind of pressure? Can he assure us that his own people will not use their power to levy tolls on an impoverished and enfeebled Europe? Is the trade even of Great Britain or France secure? Now, it seems to me, is the time when small nations have, more than ever, to look out for themselves. Divided Russia and the congeries of independent Balkan states are sure to be exploited by united Germany, if that country can keep united; otherwise, it, too, will be subject to exploitation. They may set up custom-houses on every frontier, but great combinations of capital will exploit and subjugate them all the same.

And it is in this new world of fierce competition and exploitation we are being assured that, thrown on ourselves, we in Ireland can hold our own: we who were not able to hold it in the easy-going world of the past. It is a question of business; which, however, should be fairly clear even to a child.

8. *A Question of Business.*—Great Britain, with all her resources, will find it very difficult to hold her trade in the new era. But, even loaded as she is with debt, she is in ever so much a better position than we; with our poverty, lack of resources, and of industrial and commercial experience. There is only one way in which we could hope to better ourselves by separating from Britain—by continuing to share in the fruits of her trade, without doing our part to maintain it: taking of the profits

without paying the price. If permitted, it might succeed for a time, but would surely lead to ruin ultimately. In any case, it is not the way of honour.

Let these islands do their very best,—standing loyally back to back, dealing equal justice, man and master making equal sacrifice,—and still they will find it hard to live and keep their trade in the days that anyone can see coming. Let us pull against one another,—Labour against Employers, Briton against Irishman; each striving to get the other to bear more than his share of the common burthen,—and we are all sure to go down together. Should the trade of Britain fail,—as is but too possible,—I do not know how ours is to maintain itself. And I, for one, do not want the Self-Determination that is allowed to rule a bare cupboard and an empty purse.

CHAPTER IX

OF THE PRINCIPLE OF HOME RULE; AND OF COLONIAL HOME RULE

1. *Majority Rule.*—In England, France, the United States, and all democratic countries, the holders of power are elected by the people; that is, by the majority; and it is a further democratic principle that "minorities must suffer", in the sense of being ruled by those whom, if they could, they would deprive of power. The consent of the governed, in this way, becomes the consent of the majority; while minorities are ruled against their will. They consent, if you like, conditionally— rather than break away or leave the country. But would they be allowed to break away? Practically, they are forced to stay and submit to alien rule.

2. *Local Self-Government.*—To relieve this hardship, local affairs are put, almost universally, under control of the people of the place; as it will often happen that those who are in a minority in the nation have a majority, and consequent local authority, in their own district. Unionists, for instance, have ruled Birmingham for many years, while Liberals held the national government at Westminster; and, conversely, Liberals have held Manchester during Unionist administrations. Democrats may rule at Washington, while Pennsylvania is controlled by Republicans; and the Governor of New York State may be a Republican while a Democrat is Mayor of the City. In Ireland, Dublin, Cork, and other towns, besides four-fifths of the county and district councils, are in the hands of Nationalists; while the central authority, in Dublin Castle, is held by men who were appointed from Westminster. Nay, while the City of Dublin is ruled by a Nationalist corporation, some of the

suburban districts—Rathmines and Pembroke—have Unionist councils. Minorities thus come in for a share of power,—where they form a local majority,—in any place that is important enough to be allowed to rule itself. Self-rule, in this sense, is practically universal; in countries that are governed more or less despotically, as well as in the most democratic republics.

This arrangement, though serving to relieve the hardship of minorities, does not bring relief to all; as there are people who, though numerous, educated, wealthy, and very able, have a majority nowhere, practically. Where, for instance, is any government in the hands of Jews? Individuals of the race, no doubt, hold office in many governments; but not as Jews. They have been elected, or selected, as Liberals, Conservatives, Labour Leaders, or Socialists. As Hebrew Nationalists they rule nowhere; though, perhaps, they may soon be allowed to rule again in Palestine, if they form a majority therein.

3. *Home Rule.*—When, therefore, it is laid down as a demo-cratic principle that majorities must rule and minorities be ruled, it is understood with the important limitation that minorities shall be allowed Home Rule where they form a majority; in so far as the place in question is entitled to self-government. In Germany, Bavarians rule Bavaria; Saxons, Saxony: that is, in matters purely Bavarian or Saxon. Each of the United States is ruled by its own people. In the British Empire, Canada is ruled by Canadians; Australia by Australians; South Africa by South Africans; and so on. The British Islands show remnants of their old separate governments: in the administration of justice, for instance, education, many branches of finance, and other matters; which, in the case of Scotland, are governed from Edinburgh; and in that of Ireland, from Dublin Castle, for the whole of this country.

It is partial Home Rule, already in existence and working well. In Ireland this central authority is not in the hands of representatives of the Irish people; who, in this way, are deprived of local control of the government. Therein is the grievance of which Irish Home Rulers complain.

The complaint must be deemed just, provided the people of Ireland are so advanced in culture as to be capable of self-government; and provided also they may be trusted to make legitimate use of it—not as an instrument of pressure, to secure a larger measure of independence than is their due. In Canada, for instance, the French of the province of Quebec have powers that are denied to the Indians; but even the French Canadians would not be allowed to form a separate and independent republic. So, too, in the United States; in South Africa, with the Negroes; in Australia, with the Bushmen; in New Zealand, with the Maoris. No Irish Nationalist, if he had to deal practically with those races, would give them the same amount of self-rule as French Canadians enjoy.

In Hindustan it is different; as the natives there have an old and highly developed civilisation. The question, however, is whether they are capable of self-rule as a united people; and whether, short of that, they can be trusted to make a just and moderate use of local government, without abusing it to tyrannise over minorities, or making it into an instrument of pressure to secure a degree of national independence which would be their undoing. This, I take it, is the real question with which the Imperial Government in India has to deal: whether and how far the subject peoples are capable of and therefore entitled to self-government. It is not to be solved by the simple formula that self-government, whether complete or local, is the right of all people whatsoever. No one in his senses believes in that.

4. *Conflicting Principles.*—Accordingly, here again we find principles, not only political but ethical, which, if not judiciously handled, may come into conflict; with disastrous results, whichever should unduly prevail. Self-government is right and due where and in so far as the people concerned are ripe for it, by development; and where and in so far as it does not interfere with any larger union which, as we have seen, the law of development may require. Such union also is no less right and natural, where it makes for prosperity; but, even so, it should not interfere with local self-government, in so far as the people are ripe for this, and will not abuse it.

It is easy to conceive how, in harmonising these principles, mistakes and conflicts may arise, even among the most upright statesmen; some fearing that a people may not be yet sufficiently developed to be entrusted with this or that measure of self-rule; or that the amount of self-rule they demand is incompatible with the authority that is requisite for central government. Others may fear the opposite: that the central authority may be unduly cramping the people's faculties, by keeping them in leading-strings; either denying them self-government in any shape, or unduly limiting the authority which it allows.

It is not for ethics, primarily, to determine the proportion in which both these principles should be applied in any particular case, to secure the true balance of which that case is capable. It is a question of business—statesmanship: what precise amount of freedom and of limitation makes for prosperity with a people of this kind, in circumstances like these. Ethics accepts and ratifies the conclusion at which statesmanship arrives. And though I do not regard it as belonging to my branch of study to determine whether, for instance, the legislative union of these islands, which I am disposed to look on as making for the prosperity not only of Britain but of Ireland,—is compatible, say, with what is known as Colonial Home Rule; I may, perhaps, be allowed to make some remarks, in what, I hope, shall be modest criticism, of certain recent statements that have been made thereon.

5. *Colonial Home Rule, for Colonies.*—Home Rule, as the British Colonies enjoy it, comprises freedom from legal obligation to contribute (1) money to the Imperial Exchequer; or (2) soldiers for the defence of the Empire. The Colonies, moreover, are empowered (3) to negotiate their own commercial arrangements with foreign countries, and to set up customs barriers on their frontiers and at their ports, so that ships and persons entering may be searched for articles liable to duty. There is, perhaps, a non-legal obligation,—of piety, taken in the strict sense,—to contribute to the support of the mother country, which, however, has no right to enforce the least contribution.

Now, I notice, in the first place, that the colonies of Great Britain are peculiarly favoured in being allowed freedom of this kind. The states that make the German Empire enjoyed it when they made war on France in 1870; but Bismarck evidently thought it incompatible with the strength deriving from unity which he wished for the Fatherland; and Bismarck was a master of statecraft. In Italy also the different petty kingdoms and republics enjoyed it for centuries, during which Austria, France, and Spain could overrun them at pleasure. It is different now that they have a common army, exchequer, and fiscal system. Could there be a common army, if the others were not common? Great Britain also has proved herself strong; but if the ancient kingdoms of which she is composed,— England, Scotland, and Wales; not to speak of the smaller divisions of each,—were allowed colonial Home Rule, they would go down easily in the next war with any really united country. And Scotland and Wales are nations; or once were.

6. *Nationalist Demand at Convention.*—Secondly, I notice that of the Nationalist members of the late Convention, the more advanced section, though demanding colonial Home Rule, did not mean, as I understand, that it should be as full as that which is enjoyed by the colonies. In the report which that group of the Convention presented, they admitted that, for purposes of naval defence, "Ireland must be considered as integrally connected with Great Britain, so that defence must be by one force, under one control". As regards the army, while a few of the group agreed that "in time of war or imminence of war all military forces and organisations in the United Kingdom must pass under the. absolute control of the Imperial Authorities"; the majority, though present, did not vote on the question. Canadians or Australians would have had no such difficulty in making up their minds.

In respect of finance, all recognised, "without question", "the obligation of Ireland to contribute according to her means" to imperial services; and, "in view of strong Unionist feeling", they agreed to make this "a statutory payment, to be fixed provisionally at the outset, and afterwards by agreement between the Imperial and Irish Governments". No such payment is made by the colonies.

It seems to me, therefore, that, while demanding colonial Home Rule, these Nationalists did not mean that it should be fully colonial; but only freedom to contribute less for Imperial purposes than we do at present. Admitting all the principles of the Unionists, they differed only as regards amounts. It was a difference that should have been capable of settlement by arbitration, as the Imperial Parliament proposed.

Even the advanced Nationalists, therefore, were content to insist (1) that Ireland's contribution of soldiers in time of war would be determined solely by her own Parliament, as in the colonies; and (2) on her "right to guard her own trade interests and control her own trade policy". This meant power to establish a customs tariff different from that of Britain and it was on this rock the Convention ultimately went to pieces.

7. *Control of Customs.*—Those who made the demand, pleaded that "as both countries are so deeply interested in free access to one another's markets, we believe that mutual advantage would be a surer guarantee of free and friendly intercourse than any legal restrictions. But, in order to meet Unionist fears, we are ready to agree to provisions in the Constitutional Act maintaining free trade between the two countries in articles of home produce, subject to safeguards against dumping, for a reasonable number of years, and thereafter by mutual agreement. This would ensure that if any change became absolutely necessary, owing either to an altered tariff policy in Great Britain, or to any other reason, it could not be made without prolonged deliberation in the Irish Parliament.

The two countries would at once have different tariffs in respect of foreign imports, with a possibility of a tariff war between Ireland and Britain after a term of years, undefined.

Here the question of business, underlying that of ethics, is, whether this would make for such unity as is required by the law of development. The signatories to this report plead, further, that "it may be said with truth that the power of each state within the Empire to control the whole of its own taxation, and especially its customs, is the very corner-stone of Imperial Unity". Is it not rather, in so far as it exists,—for it does not exist between the nations that compose Britain,—the source of whatever looseness and weakness there is in the constitution of the British Empire? How Bismarck would have mocked at a proposal to allow each of the German states its own customs tariff and full control of its own taxation, as the best means of securing the unity and strength of the Imperial Bund.

8. *Do Separate Tariffs Make for Imperial Strength?*—To me it seems unquestionable that independence in respect of tariffs, however advantageous to the colonies of Britain, does not make for the unity and strength of the Empire; and that, similarly, the power and prosperity of the United Kingdom would diminish if there were separate tariffs between its constituent parts. This is held to be manifest as regards England, Scotland, and Wales.

Ireland, no doubt, as the report which I have been quoting insists, is like the colonies in this, that it is separated entirely by water from Britain. So is Sicily from Italy; but are the colonies so dependent as we on the English market? Have they no better prospect of being able, some day, to cut the Imperial connection and do for themselves? If I saw parallelism in these respects, I think I should deem it the interest of the colonies to draw closer to the United Kingdom, by adopting her fiscal policy, rather than advise the Irish people to press for the separated fiscal policy of the colonies. That is, if I deemed the colonies as closely united by nature to the mother country as Ireland is to England. Trade interests are stronger than any bond of blood; and are at their strongest when, in any great Imperial combination, the constituent parts enjoy equal rights, with common protection against alien competition.

9. *Risk in Common Tariff.*—In such a combination, no doubt, the weaker parts are liable to be out-voted and to get foul play; as, there is good reason to believe, has been Ireland's lot in the past. We should have had to face this risk if we were to accept the proposal made to the Convention by the Prime Minister—of a thorough revision of the whole question after the war.

Even so, the Unionist members thought it worth taking, for the commercial advantages which whole-hearted union with England would bring; directly to her; and, through her, to us. These Unionists were business men of great experience; who, though prejudiced in many ways, have a keen eye to their own commercial interests. They pay as much of the Imperial taxes, in proportion, as we; very likely more; as they have larger business and are wealthier; while taxation is falling more and more on wealth. Yet, looking at the present fiscal arrangement,—of community of customs,—as a matter of business, they deemed the prosperity which it secures us, through Britain, worth the risk which it involves. Though liable to be out-voted, we could make a fight for our rights; and there is not an empire, kingdom, or republic anywhere, that would not split up at once, if the various parts refused to take this kind of risk.

CHAPTER X

OF MAJORITY RULE AND
THE ULSTER QUESTION

1. *PRINCIPLES to be Harmonised.*—We have already seen how the principle that Majorities must rule, is to be accepted subject to the limitation that Minorities must be allowed local self-rule, where they form a majority. I propose to consider here more in detail how these principles may be harmonised.

For illustration, we will take the case of the United Kingdom; which is under the rule of a common Parliament, wherein Irishmen complain that they are in a permanent minority. The Scotch, however, and the Welsh are in the same position; and it has been known that a considerable majority of the representatives of England were in a minority at Westminster; the majority there being made up of a minority of English Liberals, reinforced by a majority of those from Scotland, Wales, and Ireland Every one admits that, in the common Parliament, the majority of representatives elected by the whole United Kingdom must rule for the Imperial matters that come under its jurisdiction.

Together with the central government at Westminster, having jurisdiction over the whole of Great Britain and Ireland, there have been from time immemorial governing bodies with jurisdiction restricted to their own districts. Such were the city and town corporations, and the grand juries of the counties. These, like the central Parliament, were for long elected on a narrow franchise; but now all are democratised, so as to rest on the votes of the majority of those whom they control.

In addition to the local bodies just mentioned, there have been, and are, central governments, with jurisdiction over the whole of each of the Kingdoms that form the Union, but restricted to some one of these. In Ireland, for instance, the jurisdiction of the Lord Lieutenant and all that we mean by Dublin Castle, extends over the whole of the kingdom, but not beyond. The Home Rule demand, whatever shape it took, whether for Repeal of the Union or the something less that would have satisfied Butt and Parnell,—was, in effect, that this central Irish government should be democratised, and made to rest on the majority of the votes of the Irish people; instead of, as it does, on a majority in the Imperial Parliament, wherein Irish representatives are a minority. The demand was, therefore, to the effect that a minority of the United Kingdom should rule in that part of the Union in which they are a majority.

Here, accordingly, we find another principle, modifying that of majority rule: to wit, that Local governments should rule by consent of the majority of those whom they govern; even though these should differ, in politics and otherwise, from the majority of some larger place or kingdom in which the district in question is contained. It may, therefore, be said with truth that democratic local government, in every form, is based on the principle of minority rule, as well as on that of government by the majority. This applies, not only to Home Rule for Ireland, but to whatever local government there may be, in any place whatsoever.

2. *Minorities must be Ruled.*—It maybe well to note that the principle does not apply to those who form but a minority in any realm or district; as the Catholic Celts of Belfast or Liverpool, the Protestant Anglo-Saxons of Dublin or Cork. If, indeed, they should be a majority in some electoral division,—as in the Falls or Rathmines,—they elect their own representatives, and if the district in question should be entitled to a district or other council, they rule therein.

3. *The Common Local Government which we Call Home Rule.*— Moreover, among other arguments whereon in Ireland we used to base the Home Rule claim, we were wont to insist on homogeneity and diversity of race, mentality, religion, and culture generally; homogeneity, for Ireland; and diversity, from the remainder of the United Kingdom. We argued that, while

Ireland differs very much from Britain, within our own seas
we are all Irish, with substantially the same ideals and outlook
on life. Thereby we implied another principle, to the effect that,
Where a number of contiguous minor districts, each entitled
to and enjoying local government, are inhabited by people
who agree in race and culture among themselves, but differ
from their neighbours, they are entitled to a common government for the region taken as a whole; provided always the
homogeneous districts of which the region is composed are
contiguous. On this principle we claimed a common government for the Irish in Ireland, but without jurisdiction over
those in Glasgow, Liverpool, London, or New York. These,
being in separated districts, must submit to be governed therein.

4. *Application to Ulster.*—In due time came the retort of the
Ulster Protestants, whereby our sincerity was tested. They said:
We, too, are a people differing in race, religion, mentality, culture, ideals, and the rest, from you, Catholic Celts, who dwell
in the rest of Ireland. We control Belfast, it is true, as well as
the other districts wherein we are the majority; but, on your
own principle, we have a right to more. You are not content
with the power which you have in Dublin, Cork, Limerick,
and the other cities, counties, and districts of the South, East,
and West; you want common local government, which you
call Home Rule. We want the same, for the cities and counties
which we hold. In other words, we want Home Rule for Ulster.

Nationalists have been wont to meet this demand by
insisting on majority rule; as if Home Rule did not consist
essentially in rule by minorities, wherever they form a majority.
We question the fact that Protestant Anglo-Saxons are a
majority in Ulster; but surely there is no denying that they are
a homogeneous majority in the north-east corner. Sometimes,
in a half-hearted way, we try to argue that these northern
Protestants are Irishmen, just like ourselves; that, therefore,
they cannot show that homogeneity and diversity on which we
base the claim for Home Rule. They, however, have voted
differently, and consistently, for a hundred years; thereby
showing that in race, culture, religion, and mentality, they and
we are different.

Were Ireland made a republic fully independent of Great Britain, it seems to me that she would be bound to allow Home Rule to the north-east corner; on the principles that underlie the claim we make for Home Rule in the United Kingdom, which I regard as well-founded. The Protestants of Ulster differ from the majority in the rest of the island, not only in religion, but in race, mentality, culture generally. They are at once homogeneous and heterogeneous: homogeneous in their own districts, of which many are contiguous; heterogeneous, as compared with the rest of Ireland. A minority in Ireland, they are a majority in the north-east corner; and therefore, on the principles which we have been advocating, are entitled to Home Rule.

5. *Limitation of the Ulster Claim.*—This, however, should not be allowed except in the districts where they have a majority. Not, therefore, in the whole of Ulster; nor even in the whole of the six counties which they claim. It should be easy to determine where they have a majority; and so far their Home Rule should extend, even though it might be necessary to break up some of the present counties. These are not so ancient or indigenous that we should fight to the death rather than allow them to undergo any substantial change.

6. *Separation.*—Meanwhile it is curious to note how the Nationalists, who, for claiming Home Rule, were dubbed Separatists, and who complained of this, came themselves to denounce as Separatists those who would allow Home Rule to the Protestants of Ulster, even for a time; while both Ulster Protestants and Nationalists, from claiming the local government which was their due, allowed themselves to be pushed by extremists into demanding real separation. Sinn Féin would separate completely from Britain; while the Ulster supporters of Sir Edward Carson would separate as completely from the rest of Ireland. Both are wrong; erring, practically, in the same way.

CHAPTER XI

OF THE BASIS OF TAXATION; AND OF
THE FINANCIAL RELATIONS BETWEEN
GREAT BRITAIN AND IRELAND.

1. *THE Question, in Relation to Ireland.*—I have called attention to the real danger involved in fiscal union of Ireland and Great Britain—that Ireland, being in a minority in the Imperial Parliament, may be out-voted in regard to taxation, and so made to bear an undue share of the common burthen. Inequity of this kind might be so great as to more than counter-balance any good which may come from the Union, in the way of trade. And as there is good reason for thinking that, through inequitable tariffs, we were made to pay a great deal more than our fair share in the past, no patriotic Irishman can advocate the Union till he has been satisfied that this tariff system has been righted so as to make the scales balance fairly; or, at least, not lean so heavily against us as to deprive us of whatever benefit, by way of increase of trade, the Union may bring.

No one likes taxation; and few are satisfied that they are not charged with more than their due proportion. In recent years, however, two classes seem to have taken up the cry with special warmth, so as, in a sense, to make the grievance their own. Wage-earners, now become Socialists, almost everywhere; and Irish Nationalists of all grades, rich as well as poor. Extreme Socialists find herein a justifying cause for revolution, against Capitalist or Bourgeois government; while for advanced Irish Nationalists over-taxation of their country is one of the main grievances on which they rely to justify whatever resistance, active or passive, they make to the present Government.

Here, again, the student of ethics, however expert, has little competence, as such, and must seek guidance from one of the ancillary sciences. Whatever mode of levying taxes makes for the good of the commonwealth, is right ethically; and that is about all that ethics, as such, can say on the matter. It is for political economy to decide whether a certain budget satisfies the condition—makes for the national welfare or the reverse. And as I am not an economist, I can discuss the question only very cursorily and with great reserve; venturing merely some modest criticism of statements which I find advanced by others—economists, Socialists, and Irish Nationalists.

2. *Report of the Childers Commission.*—Two official documents are of cardinal importance: the Report of the Childers Commission, and the Finance Act of 1894, popularly known as Sir William Harcourt's Death Duties Budget.

The Commission was appointed in that year, "to inquire into the financial relations between Great Britain and Ireland, and their relative taxable capacity". They were asked to report, among other things, "upon what principles of comparison, and by the application of what specific standards, the relative capacity of Great Britain and Ireland to bear taxation may be most equitably determined". The very question with which we are concerned.

In its early stages, while the Commission was taking evidence, its Chairman was the Right Hon. H. C. E. Childers, who had been Chancellor of the Exchequer in a Liberal Government; and who must, therefore, be regarded as an expert in public finance. He died before any report was presented; but, fortunately, before his death, had prepared the draft of a report, which was, to a very large extent, the basis of nearly all the reports of his colleagues. There were seven of these reports, besides the draft just mentioned; such was the disagreement among the thirteen members of the Commission. All, however, except one,[1] agreed with Mr. Childers that Ireland had long

---

[1] Sir Thomas Sutherland, M.P. Another, Sir David Barbour; agreed conditionally: "if the proportion of revenue to be raised from Ireland is to be regulated solely by a reference to the 'taxable capacity' of the two countries". From n. 41, however, and certain other statements in his report, I gather that Sir David would take something besides "taxable capacity" into account in apportioning taxes.

been made to bear an undue share of the burthen of taxation; the annual excess, at the time of the Commission, being something between two and three million pounds sterling. Three of the Irish members were disposed to rate it higher.

3. *Overtaxation Coincident with Poverty.*—The general estimate was based on the admitted fact that Ireland is a poor country, as compared to England; with the result that, while taxes are levied according to the same rules on both, they pressed more severely on Ireland, because they pressed more severely on the poor everywhere, even in Great Britain.

This, I understand, is part of the Socialistic contention: that the poor are taxed too heavily, in England as in Ireland; while the rich in Ireland get off easily, like those of their class in the sister island. Instead, therefore, of passing special laws for Ireland in this matter, statesmen should introduce reform all round, in Great Britain as in Ireland, in full assurance that the poor of Ireland, like those of their class everywhere, would thereby secure equal justice.

Something like this seems to have appealed with great force to Sir David Barbour and Sir Thomas Sutherland; each of whom presented a special report which will repay study; especially that of Sir David Barbour, an Irishman of great administrative experience in finance. To me also, as one not versed in such matters, the argument appeals for serious consideration; calling, I think, for reply from those in Ireland who complain of overtaxation. Were we allowed Colonial Home Rule or full independence to-morrow, our poor would still have grievous cause of complaint, did we continue to levy taxes as they were raised in the United Kingdom down to the time of the Childers Commission.

4. *Change Introduced by Sir William Harcourt.*—Since then, however, a change has taken place that should not be left out of sight in any review of the whole question. From a Note attached to one of the special reports presented by members of the Childers Commission,[2] we learn that the latest financial

---

[2] That which was signed by The O'Connor Don (who succeeded Mr. Childers in the chair), Mr. J. E. Redmond, and three others. *Final Report, p.* 16.

returns available at the time were those for 1893–4; the very year before Sir William Harcourt passed the Death Duties Budget that revolutionised taxation; introducing a wedge that tends more and more to throw the burthen on the wealthy. With this result, as regards Ireland, that in the years immediately preceding the great war, our country, being poor, was run at a loss to England. The balance, of between two and three millions or more against us, had disappeared; and had even been appearing on the other side. This, I understand, is acknowledged as a fact; but I doubt whether its significance is recognised as it should be.

Given the fact, if England refused us the fiscal independence she allows the colonies, it could not be for any direct pecuniary tribute she wrung from us; and, conversely, a demand for colonial Home Rule on our part would not have been then reasonably based on the ground that, under the Union, we were overtaxed for the benefit of Great Britain. Seeing that we no longer gave to that island,—at least directly, in the way of taxation,—we should have looked at home and seen whether consumers of taxed commodities were not paying more than their due; more than they need have paid if owners of property,—including shopkeepers and farmers,—and those who draw good salaries,—including professors and writers on politics,—were taxed to their full capacity. So, I expect, a Socialist, even of moderate type, would regard the question.

That was before the war; when the Imperial burthen was light, compared to what it has since become. One who thinks, as I do, that it is still the interest of Ireland to unite with and support Great Britain, will have to admit, logically, that we should pay our fair share of the Imperial taxes. Even the more advanced Nationalist members of the Convention admitted this, as we have seen. What our fair share may now be I do not know; nor, I fear, does anyone.[3] I should like, however,

---

[3] Owing to the immense load of debt remaining from the war, it is very possible that the whole fiscal system of these countries will have to be recast. At any rate, it is hard to see how severe indirect taxation can be avoided; though, as has been said, this falls heaviest on the poor, and was thereby the main cause of the

to see some reasonable proof that those in Ireland who have wealth should not contribute to the Imperial burthen at the same rate as those of the same class in Britain.

5. *Basis of Taxation: Duties on Commodities.*—This leads to another aspect of the question: whether, in apportioning taxes, equity demands that one should have regard only to means; without considering indirect results—the benefit, for instance, that industry and commerce may derive from taxation of any drug or practice that makes for idleness or extravagance, or acts injuriously on the health and producing power of the citizens; those even who, having nothing superfluous, may be inclined to spend what they have unprofitably.

All the members of the Childers Commission agreed that it was the indirect taxes, from customs and excise,—which means, practically, duties on whiskey, beer, tobacco, tea, and sugar,—that pressed so hard on Ireland. The few rich people we have got off light, with those of the same class in Britain.

overtaxation of Ireland. In the new conditions, left by the war, I find it hard to complain of the Prime Minister's proposal, to the Convention, that "during the period of the war and for a period of two years thereafter, the control of Customs and Excise should be reserved to the United Kingdom Parliament; that, as soon as possible after the Irish Parliament has been established, a Joint Exchequer Board should be set up to secure the determination of the true revenue of Ireland—a provision which is essential to a system of responsible Irish Government and to the making of a national balance sheet; and that, at the end of the war; a Royal Commission should be established to re-examine impartially and thoroughly the financial relations of Great Britain and Ireland, to report on the contribution of Ireland to Imperial expenditure, and to submit proposals as to the best means of adjusting the economic and fiscal relations of the two countries".

Even the advanced section of the Nationalist members of the Convention admitted the obligation of Ireland to contribute "according to her means" to Imperial services. This meant paying her fair share of the National Debt, including the War Debt. She was "willing to agree to a statutory payment" for this purpose. But without some such Commission as the Prime Minister suggested, how could anyone now determine what is Ireland's fair share of this Imperial burthen?

There, as with us, it was the poor who were overcharged, by reason of those duties on commodities. Should, then, such taxes be abolished wholly?

Mr. Thomas Sexton, M.P., in his report, leaves one under the impression that, in his opinion, no taxes should be levied off those who have only just sufficient income to provide necessaries, for an average family. That is,—supposing necessaries to cost, on the average, £12 a head per annum; and the average family to consist of five persons,—no tax should be levied off those who have not more than £60 a year. As long, I take it, as there are any rich people left, who have not been taxed down to the £60 level.

This may not be a perfectly fair presentation of the principle of apportionment advocated by Mr. Sexton, who bases his opinion on the teaching of J. S. Mill; admitting, it is fair to add, that "it is difficult, within the limits of one country, to apply the principle, even approximately, in taxing the means of individuals". If, for instance, you place a tax on whiskey or beer, how are you to discriminate, among those who call for a glass or a pint, between such as have and such as have not a weekly income of one-pound-three-and-a-fraction? Or would you give a man his glass, if he said he had a pound a week but no wife, or no children, or but one or two? You would have to do away altogether with the whiskey and beer tax; and the same applies to all commodities.

Now, are we prepared to leave all these untaxed—whiskey, wine, beer, tobacco, tea, and such things? I do not ask whether it would be good for morals: no State that minds its own business is now supposed to care for such things. But would it make for progress—industry, prosperity, money generally? A State, one supposes, has to provide for these, however it may abstract from ethics and religion. On purely utilitarian and commercial grounds I would not abolish taxes on alcoholic drink; even though the result is sure to be that plenty of children and women will be deprived of great part of that £12 allowance; swilled up by loving husbands and fathers, in the shape of beer and whiskey. I would not let even the pipe go free; nor the tea-pot. But, then, I am not only a total abstainer but eschew tobacco and tea; so, of course, my vote counts for nothing.

6. *Taxation of Luxuries.*—Less extreme men deem these things necessary; in moderation, of course. Would you, then, tax them at least when used immoderately? And are you sure that this would not result in placing on the poor an undue share of the burthen of taxation? Many, even of the Socialists, would have no hesitation in taxing luxuries: motor-cars, yachts, race-horses, wines, cigars, and such things. But is not even bread a luxury, beyond a certain amount? Meat is, certainly; and tea, tobacco, beer and whiskey, when taken immoderately. So that, if you tax luxuries, everything will have to pay duty; and you will have to discriminate between households that really want a gallon or more and those which should not get more than a pint. And so of individuals.

I can see but one way out: to put every one on rations, of everything; thorough-going Socialism. Which, however it may result in keeping the citizens good children, may leave them only children; lacking the grit that makes so much for national prosperity. I deem the other danger the less—taxed commodities; even with the certainty that a duty on beer and such things is likely to press with undue severity on the poor. It is most regrettable; but they must bear this burthen, if they will not abstain; whether they belong to Ireland or Great Britain.

7. *Possible Mode of Adjustment.*—Only I think it fair that, as taxes of this kind are not levied so much for revenue as to diminish idleness and extravagance and to promote efficiency,— or, at least, in so far as they are not levied for revenue,—they should be spent, as far as possible, on the class from which they are derived—in promoting positive helps to secure thrift and efficiency. Others, no doubt, besides those who get themselves taxed would reap the benefit; but some, at least, of the positive helps would reach the wives and children whose share had been so badly spent originally.

On the same principle, or some one closely akin, whatever inequitable super-tax may have to be levied on the poor, of either Great Britain or Ireland, should be devoted, as far as possible, to local purposes. And as people so fully developed as the Irish are likely to do this more wisely and economically, if left to do it themselves, they should, I fancy, have the spending of these moneys. Which is but part of the claim of Ireland, England, Scotland, and Wales to what we call Home Rule in Ireland.

All of which, however, has to be fitted in with the principle that each unit of the Empire must pay its fair share of the Imperial taxes. Should wealth not suffice for this, without unduly limiting capital, and thereby cramping industry, part of the burthen must fall on the poor. How much, it is only experience can determine. Absolute Socialism,—if it could be secured,—might lead to equality of taxes; but it might also lead to evils greater than those from which we suffer at present.

NOTES

I

EXTRACTS FROM LETTERS OF THE PRIME MINISTER, MR. D. LLOYD GEORGE, PROPOSING HOME RULE FOR IRELAND, WITH CONDITIONS OF THE SAME[1]

i

Prime Minister to Mr. Redmond

10, Downing Street,
"Whitehall, S.W.1.
"16*th May*, 1917.

"The idea of the Government has been to try to effect an immediate settlement, conceding the largest measure of Home Rule which can be secured by agreement at this moment, without prejudice to the undertaking by Parliament of a further and final settlement of the questions most in dispute, after the war. They are therefore prepared to put forward proposals on the following lines, with a view to present action.

Firstly, they would introduce a Bill for the immediate application of the Home Rule Act to Ireland, but excluding therefrom the six counties of North-East Ulster, such exclusion to he subject to reconsideration by Parliament at the end of five years, unless it is previously terminated by the action of the Council of Ireland, to be set up as hereinafterwards described.

[1] See the *Final Report of the Proceedings of the Irish Convention*, pp. 20, 50.

"Secondly, with a view to securing the largest possible measure of common action for the whole of Ireland, the Bill would provide for a Council of Ireland to be composed of two delegations, consisting, on the one hand, of all the members returned to Westminster from the excluded area, and, on the other, of a delegation equal in number from the Irish Parliament. This council could be summoned on the initiative of any six members. It would be empowered by a majority of votes of each of the delegations (*a*) to pass private Bill legislation affecting both the included and the excluded area; (*b*) to recommend to the Crown the extension to the excluded area by Order in Council of any Act of the Irish Parliament; (*c*) to agree to the inclusion under the Home Rule Act of the whole of Ireland, subject to the assent of the majority of the votes in the excluded area, power to be vested in the Crown in that case to extend the Act to all Ireland by Order in Council; (*d*) to make recommendations on its own initiative upon Irish questions, including the amendment of the Home Rule Act as finally passed. . . .

"Thirdly, the Government consider that the financial proposals of the Home Rule Act are unsatisfactory and ought to be reconsidered. There are a number of important objects, such as the development of Irish industries, the improvement of housing in the towns, and the furtherance of education (including a better scale of remuneration for teachers), which cannot, owing to changed conditions which have arisen since the war, be adequately dealt with under the provisions of that Act without imposing an undue burden on the Irish taxpayer.

"Fourthly, the Government would recommend that, after second reading, the Bill embodying the above proposals, together with the Home Rule Act, should be forthwith considered by a Conference to be constituted on the lines of the Speaker's Conference on Electoral Reform, though not consisting exclusively of Members of Parliament, and meeting under the chairmanship of someone commanding the same general confidence in his impartiality and judgment as Mr. Speaker himself. The Conference would, of course, have full power to suggest any alterations in the Government scheme upon which it might decide.

"The Government feel that a proposal which provides for immediate Home Rule for the greater part of Ireland, while excluding that part of Ireland which objects to coming under the Home Rule Act, for a definite period after which Parliament will consider the matter afresh; which recognises the profound sentiment existing in Ireland for the unity of the country by creating a common council to consider Irish affairs as a whole; which, finally, sets up a representative Conference to attempt to adjust the most difficult questions involved, is as far as they can possibly go towards effecting a legislative settlement in the crisis of a great war.

"They are prepared to introduce a Bill on these lines. But they feel that it would be idle, and I am sure you will agree with them, to introduce such a Bill unless it were assured of something like a second reading acceptance from both Irish parties. . . .

"We earnestly recommend the proposals which I have outlined above to the dispassionate consideration of men of all parties. If upon such consideration a basis for immediate action is found in them we shall proceed at once with the necessary steps to carry them into effect".

If the preceding Chapters contain anything like the truth, this proposal must be deemed fair. It does not, it is true, come up to the ideal regarding Ulster set forth in Chapter X.; but in real life one hardly ever finds the ideal. In my opinion, the proposal should have been accepted.

ii

Prime Minister to Sir Horace Plunkett, Chairman
of the Irish Convention

10, Downing Street,
"London, S.W.,
"25th February, 1918.

"There is a further consideration which has an important
bearing on the possibilities of the present situation. During the
period of the war it is necessary to proceed as far as possible
by agreement. Questions on which there is an acute
difference of opinion in Ireland or in Great Britain must be
held over for consideration after the war. At the same time it
is clear to the Government, in view of previous attempts at
settlement, and of the deliberations of the Convention itself,
that the only hope of agreement lies in a solution which, on
the one side, provides for the unity of Ireland under a single
Legislature with adequate safeguards for the interests of Ulster
and the Southern Unionists, and, on the other, preserves
the well-being of the Empire and the fundamental unity of the
United Kingdom.

"It is evident that there is on the part of all parties in the
Convention a willingness to provide for and safeguard the
interests of the Empire and of the United Kingdom. A settlement can now be reached which will reserve by common
consent to the Imperial Parliament its suzerainty, and its
control of Army, Navy, and Foreign Policy and other Imperial
services, while providing for Irish representation at Westminster,
and for a proper contribution from Ireland to Imperial expenditure. All these matters are now capable of being settled within
the Convention on a basis satisfactory both to the Imperial
Government and to Ireland.

"There remains, however, the difficult question of Customs
and Excise. The Government are aware of the serious objection
which can be raised against the transfer of these services to an
Irish Legislature. It would be practically impossible to make
such a disturbance of the fiscal and financial relations of

Great Britain and Ireland in the midst of a great war. It might also be incompatible with the federal reorganisation of the United Kingdom in favour of which there is a growing body of opinion. On the other hand, the Government recognise the strong claim that can be made that an Irish Legislature should have some control over indirect taxation as the only form of taxation which touches the great majority of the people, and which in the past has represented the greater part of Irish revenue.

"The Government feel that this is a matter which cannot be finally settled at the present time. They therefore suggest for the consideration of the Convention that, during the period of the war and for a period of two years thereafter, the control of Customs and Excise should be reserved to the United Kingdom Parliament; that as soon as possible after the Irish Parliament shall have been established, a Joint Exchequer Board should be set up to secure the determination of the true revenue of Ireland—a provision which is essential to a system of responsible Irish Government and to the making of a national balance sheet, and that, at the end of the war, a Royal Commission should be established to re-examine impartially and thoroughly the financial relations of Great Britain and Ireland, to report on the contribution of Ireland to Imperial expenditure, and to submit proposals as to the best means of adjusting the economic and fiscal relations of the two countries.

"The Government consider that during the period of the war the control of all taxation other than Customs and Excise could be handed over to the Irish Parliament; that for the period of the war and two years thereafter an agreed proportion of the annual Imperial expenditure should be fixed as the Irish contribution; and that all Irish revenue from Customs and Excise as determined by the Joint Exchequer Board, after deduction of the agreed Irish contribution to Imperial expenditure, should be paid into the Irish Exchequer. For administrative reasons, during the period of the war it is necessary that the Police should remain under Imperial control and it seems to the Government to be desirable that for the same period the Postal service should be a reserved service.

"Turning to the other essential element of a settlement— the securing of an agreement to establish a single Legislature for an united Ireland—the Government believe that the Convention has given much thought to the method of over- coming objection on the part of Unionists, North and South, to this proposal. They understand that one scheme provides for additional representation by means of nomination or elec- tion. They understand further that it has also been suggested that a safeguard of Ulster interests might be secured by the provision of an Ulster Committee within the Irish Parliament, with power to modify, and if necessary to exclude, the application to Ulster of certain measures either of legislation or administration which are not consonant with the interests of Ulster. This appears to be a workable expedient, whereby special consideration of Ulster conditions can be secured and the objections to a single Legislature for Ireland overcome.

"The Government would also point to the fact that it has been proposed that the Irish Parliament should meet in alternate sessions in Dublin and Belfast, and that the principal offices of an Irish Department of manufacturing industry and commerce should be located in Belfast. They believe that the willingness to discuss these suggestions is clear evidence of the desire to consider any expedient which may help to remove the causes of Irish disunion. The fact that, in order to meet the claims of different parts of the community, the South African Convention decided that the Legislature was to be established in Cape Town, the Administrative Departments to be situated in Pretoria, and the Supreme Court was to sit in Bloemfontein, is a proof that proposals such as these may markedly contri- bute to eventual agreement. . . .

"There seems to be within the reach of the Convention the possibility of obtaining a settlement which will lay the foundation of a new era in the government both of Ireland and Great Britain. It is a settlement which will give to Irishmen the control of their own affairs, while preserving the funda- mental unity of the United Kingdom, and enabling Irishmen to work for the good of the Empire as well as for the good of

Ireland. With all the earnestness in their power the Government appeal to the members of the Convention to agree upon a scheme which can be carried out at once and which will go a long way towards realising the hope of Irishmen all over the world, without prejudice to the future consideration of questions on which at present agreement cannot be attained in Ireland and which are also intimately connected with constitutional problems affecting every part of the United Kingdom, the consideration of which must be postponed till the end of the present war. This is an opportunity for a settlement by consent that may never recur, and which, if it is allowed to pass, must inevitably entail consequences for which no man can wish to make himself responsible.

Another fair proposal, as it seems to me; and coming nearer to the ideal as regards Ulster. An Ulster Committee within the Irish Parliament would not be far removed from Home Rule for that part of the island. It would be much better than the undemocratic and inequitable proposition for additional representation of Irish Unionists; which, by reason of its undemocratic character, the Ulster representatives of that party rejected as "wholly unacceptable". The demand for full fiscal autonomy was the rock on which the Convention split. In the circumstances of the war, and with the new pile of debt, involving no one knows what new devices of taxation, the Government proposal of delay seems not unreasonable.

II

EXTRACT FROM THE REPORT OF ULSTER UNIONIST DELEGATES TO THE IRISH CONVENTION

"When the Clause claiming Fiscal Autonomy for Ireland was reached, it soon became evident that no real approach towards agreement was possible. It is clear that Fiscal Autonomy including the control of Customs and Excise and National taxation is valued by the Nationalists not only on the ground of supposed economic advantage but as an essential symbol of National independence. In opposition to this Ulster takes a firm stand on the basis of the people's common prosperity, and maintains that the Fiscal unity of the United Kingdom must be preserved intact, carrying with it as it does the Sovereignty of the Imperial Parliament and due representation therein.

"The important question of how far Ireland should contribute to Imperial taxation raised much controversy. In the earlier stages of the discussions some prominent Nationalists stated quite frankly that they recognised no responsibility for any portion of the pre-war National Debt, nor for the present war expenditure, whilst we claimed that in justice and in honour Ireland must continue to pay her full share of both. The majority of the Nationalists declined to admit such liability.

"During the financial year just ended Ireland's Imperial contribution will, it is estimated amount to about thirteen millions sterling, and possibly to twenty millions next year. An important section of the Nationalists objected to any Imperial contribution being paid, but the larger number favoured a contribution ranging from two and a half to four and a half millions sterling per annum. It was invariably a condition that the contribution should be purely voluntary and at the pleasure of the Irish Parliament. We listened to these suggestions with keen disappointment, knowing of no reason why Ireland, which is abundantly prosperous, should not in the hour of the Empire's need contribute her full share of men and money. We have always contended that there should be equality of sacrifice in every part of the United Kingdom.

"As already pointed out, a further clause in the Bishop of Raphoe's Scheme with which we found it impossible to agree claimed that compulsory Military Service could not be imposed upon Ireland by Great Britain unless with the consent of the Irish Parliament, and this demand was supported by the majority of the Convention".

The representatives of Ulster wanted close union with Great Britain, on purely business grounds; and were prepared to pay the price, in blood and money. It will be said,—and, I fear, can be said with reason,—that the Nationalists wanted the advantage of proximity to and connection with the British market, at half-price. The narrow strip of sea, they insisted, made them a colony. Sinn Féiners, more consistently, would pay nothing.

III

THE BISHOP OF RAPHOE ON IRISH TAXATION

In the draft report prepared by Mr. Childers, the taxable capacity of Ireland is represented as being at that time—in 1895—about 1/21st of that of the United Kingdom. All the members of the Commission agreed that it was not more. Three Irish members—Messrs. Sexton, Blake, and Slattery—reported that, in their opinion, it was only in the ratio, at most, of one to thirty-six.

Quite recently, the Most Rev. Dr. O'Donnell, Bishop of Raphoe, who played an important part in the Convention, presented to the Viceregal Committee of Inquiry into Irish Primary Education, a memorandum which deals with the financial relations of Great Britain and Ireland. From Treasury returns of the financial year 1916–17 he concludes that Ireland paid during that year more than £7,000,000 in excess of her due proportion of taxes.

This supposes that her taxable capacity was then 1/33rd that of Great Britain; which his Lordship thought very much above the true ratio. It would, in his opinion, be about 1/40th.

Now, it may be that the taxable capacity of Ireland, as compared with that of Britain, has diminished in this way, from the ratio of 1 to 20 at the time of the Childers Commission; with the result that the burthen presses on us more unduly now than in 1895. The basis of calculation is very uncertain: whether, that is, taxable capacity should be measured by income alone and what is taxable income. I confess myself unable to form an opinion of any value on many questions of this kind, on which the relative taxable capacity depends.

It may be, as has been said, that the capacity of Ireland is no less than in the time of the Childers Commission; but before diminishing it from 1/21st to 1/40th or even 1/33rd, I should deem the other party entitled to a hearing. Which implies that the Convention should have accepted the proposal of Mr. Lloyd George, to leave the matter for settlement after the war, when we should know the extent of the obligations of the whole United Kingdom.

PART II

Questions of War

CHAPTER I

OF PREPARATION FOR WAR: CONSCRIPTION

1. *CONSCRIPTION May be Necessary.*—It were much to be desired that there were no injustice in the world; when, of course, there would be no war, nor need there be any preparation for war. "Oh, if men were but good", exclaims Count Guido, in Browning's poem; but "they are not good". And so there is robbery, or the attempt to rob; which means war. For the Quaker's ethics never did, and never will, catch hold on men. It is the better part, no doubt, to turn the other cheek and offer even the cloak; but is it quite forbidden to knock the fellow down?

However many conscientious objectors there may be in England and elsewhere, there are few in Ireland; and none at all among the Irish Catholics who opposed conscription. They did not oppose it because they were opposed to war in any case; nor even, as far as I can discern, because they deemed the late war unjust, on the part of Britain, to whose armies they refused the conscripts.

Some of their advocates have hinted, in a shame-faced way, at a body of theological authority that regards conscription as never binding in conscience; but, to give us our due, I find it hard to think there is a theologian among us who believes that in his heart.

Like war, no doubt, conscription is very undesirable: such a pity that neighbouring nations, who are prepared to attack you, should have millions of trained soldiers to put into the field. If nations were only good; but they are not. They will have all their young men trained to war; and, when war breaks out, will call them to the colours. With the result, made ever so plain in the late struggle,—that, if you want to knock down the robber and hold your own, you must have as many trained soldiers as he. Also that it is only by conscription you can get them. The argument is simplicity itself—on the supposition that war in self-defence is right:—It is foolish and cruel to go to war without the least chance of success. There is, however, no glimpse of hope for a nation that, without conscription, fights another equally resourceful and conscript nation. Therefore,

The second premiss, I contend, was proved to demonstration in the late war.

2. *First Ground of Irish Opposition.*—"Even admitting that the cause of the Allies is clearly just, and that a law of Conscription may bind in conscience, Irish Catholics deny that the Military Service Act would so bind, if enforced in Ireland. They deny that compulsory military service may ever be imposed by one people on another; and they claim that Ireland is a distinct people from Great Britain. So Father Finlay, in "Studies".[1]

No law whatever may be imposed, nor can any tax, whether of blood or money, be rightly levied, by one people on or off another; if both are not united so as to have a common government. England cannot make laws for or tax France, nor France England. Neither could Bavaria and Prussia tax each the other before Bismarck welded them into the German Empire; after which the common government rightly subjected both to the blood-tax. Rulers at Washington could not tax Louisiana or California till these regions were brought into the Union. Now they are subject to the laws and burthens common to the States—that even of conscription.

The question, therefore, is whether Great Britain and Ireland are so united, under a common rule. What does Father Finlay say? Dr. Coffey we have heard; insinuating, through the mouth of others, that there is no such union. More cautious still is the writer in the "Theological Quarterly"; mindful of that anathema against the Fenians, which, pronounced by

[1] June 1918, p. 204.

Rome, has been repeated by so many Irish priests and bishops. One wonders, does it still hold?

3. *Second Ground.*—Father Finlay continues:—"Would Great Britain attempt to force conscription on an unwilling colony? Theoretically she has the right. She dare not attempt to exercise it".

Has she, then, the right, even theoretically? I was under the impression that the colonies were allowed to govern themselves in such matters: to make their own laws, levy their own taxes, raise their own armies. They are not as closely united with the mother country as Ireland is with Britain; nor have they, as yet, a proportionate share of votes in any common Parliament or Council. One cannot eat one's cake and have it; and neither can you retain legislative and taxing power over those to whom you have given exemption in such matters. It is, again, a question of union.

4. *Third Ground.*—"The legislatures of the colonies themselves felt bound to consult their people directly, before deciding; and South Africa and Australia have shown how, in face of a popular majority, no democratic government can impose conscription. Even in Great Britain, the consent of the people was sought, in conferences, through the labour leaders, by votes in Parliament; and it is only step by step, and always with popular approval, that conscription has been introduced and enforced. Why should Ireland be treated differently from the colonies, differently from Great Britain herself? What moral authority can the law have, when imposed upon Ireland, not only without the consent of her people, but in defiance of their passionate, almost unanimous, protest, and against the overwhelming vote of their representatives in Parliament". So Father Finlay.

They were, then, consulted, after all; they and their representatives in Parliament; and the great majority refused consent. The Conscription Act, however, was passed in compliance with the wishes of a great majority of the people of the Union. Both these are statements of fact. Is it Father Finlay's contention that no law, however just and necessary, and conformable to the wishes of a great majority of a Commonwealth, binds the citizens of any constituent country wherein the majority are opposed to the law? That unless a majority of Bavarians, for instance, wanted conscription, or war with England, they would not be bound to accept it from the majority of the German Empire or Republic? That New York, Pennsylvania, or California, if opposed to monometalism, or a tariff, or a law in restraint of trusts, is entitled to pay no heed to any enactment thereon passed in Congress? What a union that implies!

Once more the argument ignores the fact of union. It applies perfectly to the period before I 800, when Ireland had her own legislature, exchequer, military establishment. Then she might have snapped her fingers at any law or tax which the Westminster Parliament might attempt to impose upon her. It is so still, if still there is no Union. What is Father Finlay's view? What is the teaching of the Bishops and priests of Ireland; not to speak of Rome?

Even as regards Australia, does not the question remain whether the people of that country did their duty when they rejected conscription? They violated no law, it is true, binding in obedience; but did they do their duty, to the Empire or even to the Colony? Had France and Great Britain acted similarly, the German armies would be now in London, and a German fleet in Botany Bay. Did Australia, when she rejected conscription, throw part of her burthen on others? If so, how does her example help us out?

5. *The Government Dared not Enforce.*—But, it is urged, the Westminster Government yielded at length, fearing to apply conscription. The fact is so; they did yield, even to fear; but does that prove that they had no right to what they feared to enforce? "The King that fights his people fights himself": a foolish procedure. No sensible ruler wants coercion, or will have recourse to it except as a measure of necessity; and of extreme necessity, if it means shooting down the citizens. The fact that the Government yielded proves that they did not think the danger extreme, and that they had pity for a people whom they deemed unreasonable; not at all that they came to recognise that conscription was unjust as applying to Ireland.

How we forget our theology, when a principle thereof is inconvenient! A short time ago the Bishops of the Western

Church were asked by Rome for suggestions as to reform of the Canon Law; and before promulgation of the New Code, it was sent to every Bishop, for correction and renewed suggestions. Does any canonist suppose this to imply that the Code, when promulgated, would not bind without consent of the faithful or Bishops of any national church; or even against their protest? But, of course, Church and State are different; though both, they say, are God—founded.

Again, even Church rulers, at times, do not press legislation, even when just, against the continued protest of a subject people, expressed by non-observance of the law in question. But if you should take this to imply that the rulers—Pope or Bishops—regard the people as right, and their protest or refusal justified, you would show ignorance or forgetfulness of a principle laid down in every handbook of Moral Theology and Canon Law. And so, I take it, the fact that the Irish people were allowed their way, is no proof that the way was commendable.

6. *Fourth Ground of Opposition.*—"The unequal distribution of war-work has set up a number of British centres in which the young men of the country can simply laugh at conscription. We have very little corresponding in Ireland, except in the Belfast shipyards, where the valiant and magnanimous heroes, sure of exemption, have started a conscription campaign—for others. Agricultural workers would probably be exempt in Ireland, as they are in Britain; but otherwise conscription would mean here, as it does not mean in Britain, a practically clean sweep of the able-bodied manhood of the country".

So the writer in the "Irish Theological Quarterly"; who evidently betrays a consciousness that he felt the weakness of his argument. Ireland's great munition works, it has been often urged, are in the fields; where the workers "would probably be exempt". Yet there would be "a clean sweep of the manhood of the country"; the vast body of which is engaged in agriculture!

Could we not have said we were ready to give our fair share, as estimated by an Irish bureau? Therein would be some reason—some manliness; but we took our stand on nationhood, and swore that a great and ancient nation, such as ours, would not agree to have even one man sent against his will to fight for another country.

7. *How to Evade Taxes.*—If we were not bound in conscience by the Conscription Act, it could only be because the Act of Union does not bind us; whereupon may it not be urged that taxes imposed by the Imperial Parliament, against our protest,—and what taxes are imposed by that body otherwise?—do not bind us any more than the blood-tax? So that those who evade income-tax or death-duties by falsifying accounts or any other mode of fraud, however guilty of lying, would be guiltless of injustice, and may keep what they have saved in this way from the tax-collector. One wonders whether their Lordships the Bishops and the Jesuit Fathers approve of this.

In this connection I cannot refrain from entering a protest, and a caution, against what, I fear, must be regarded as the common teaching of our schools of Morals; to the effect that it is permissible to evade a good part of the taxes, direct and indirect, by false statements, false returns, falsifying accounts, and such practices. "Those", writes Father Lehmkuhl[2] "who in making a declaration of property and of the value of houses and other chattels, keep even a good deal under the value of the estate,—diminishing the price thus declared by one-fourth or one-third below the true value,—are not thereon guilty of injustice and bound to restitution. One must see, amongst other things, whether such diminution is commonly practised even by others. If so, proportion in tax-paying is already observed; nor will the Exchequer or King lack necessary taxes, seeing that these are so great and also since it is known well enough that certain arts are used by tax-payers to evade fiscal laws. In case, however, of excessive diminution of goods to be declared in this way, legal justice, at least, is violated".

This doctrine may appear in evidence in court any day and disgrace us. Any Government would, in my opinion, be justified in taking measures to put a stop to such teaching.

8. *Final Reason.*—It is hard to make sure that one has exhausted all that has been urged; but one must have pity on

---

[2] *Theol. Moral.* i. n. 1173.

readers. All opponents of conscription appealed to past, and present, misgovernment; in forms so many that it is impossible to condense the argument. Irish trade was maliciously destroyed, as it still is; there is a pampered minority, which is even allowed to threaten revolt with impunity. Their leader got a seat in the Cabinet, whereas those of the Irish were shot; the Home Rule Act, though on the Statute Book, is permanently suspended, poor as it is, in violation of the most formal pledges. And so on.

To begin with this delay of Home Rule. I understand that we could have had it for the last two years, and may have it any time, if we were content to take it for Celtic Ireland. That, however, is partition; and we who used to maintain that Home Rule for Ireland is not separation from Great Britain, now insist that Home Rule for the Saxon portion of Ulster is partition thereof from the rest of Ireland.

Then there are the broken pledges; as if responsible ministers ever promised that Ulster would not be allowed Home Rule under any Irish Parliament that might be set up. Or as if such a pledge, if given, could not be honourably withdrawn, as being opposed to the very spirit of democracy.

Then, as regards Sir Edward Carson; he, no doubt, threatened armed resistance, but did not actually resist with arms. He did not, moreover, openly ally himself, in revolt, with an enemy at war with the Empire; the most powerful that ever attacked it; the Irish revolution being timed to synchronise with England's greatest peril. Above all, Sir E. Carson did not actually shoot down four or five hundred people, soldiers and civilians. Had he done all this, perhaps he, too, would have been shot, like Messrs. Pearse and Connolly.

Besides, did Sir E. Carson threaten anything that every statesman in Europe and America would not do, in certain circumstances? He threatened revolt; but would not Mr. Asquith, Mr. Balfour, or even Lord Hugh Cecil, rebel in a cause of self-determination? Mr. J. Redmond also had enrolled, drilled, and armed volunteers; yet was offered a seat in the Cabinet. Men of sense in England did not think that preposterous. It is not to the principle of revolt they object, but only to the cause alleged; and it is but fair to Sir E. Carson and his adherents to say that the arms they procured were meant to preserve their people from subjection to an alien rule which they detest; whereas we Celts refused Home Rule when we found that it did not empower us to govern, with ourselves, another race who detest our government.

Sir E. Carson, I admit, demanded too much; for he has no right to six full counties of Ulster. Neither has he, in my opinion, a right to separate from the rest of Ireland; any more than Ireland has to separate from Great Britain. Both are entitled to local self-government or Home Rule; in subordination to the Imperial Parliament, on the part of Ireland; and to the Irish Parliament, on the part of Ulster. These are details, which should be easily arranged, if we had but the good sense and toleration to admit the principle; and were willing to allow others the right of self-determination we claim for ourselves.

9. *Reform Needed in Ireland—and Elsewhere.*—I recognise, moreover, and have endeavoured to show, that in Ireland we have real grounds of complaint—as to legislation and fiscal matters. But, then, I know of no people that are not in like position. Are there not complaints, as to unjust laws and inequitable taxation, on the part of different classes and different regions in every nation in the world? Take the Labour Party of Great Britain; or the Socialists of Germany or France; or the working-men of the United States: have they no grievances? Have French Catholics nothing of which to complain? And what would history decide as to all or any of them, if, in the time of their country's greatest need, when the invader was thundering at her gates, they had stood with folded arms and refused to defend her?

But,—and here, again, is the real issue,—Britain, it is said, is not our country; nor is her war ours. True, she is, and has been our only customer, hitherto; but the world is wide, and the seas are, or should—and shall—be free. We are independent of the English market; for we can find as good elsewhere. Our interest is that she should be impoverished and enfeebled; and so we applaud every blow she gets. Not that we want German any more than Anglo-Saxon masters; but that we hope to secure more freedom and greater wealth when England is beaten and impoverished.

If I thought this hope likely to be realised, I should not object so much; I should still contend that the north-east corner of our island was entitled to Home Rule.

I cannot, however, entertain the hope. Here, of course, I pretend to no special competence; as this aspect of the question is for men of business. Not ten such in Ireland, however, have any hope of the kind. Has Father Finlay, I wonder; or the Jesuit body; or the Bench of Bishops; or have the experienced clergy? Would they invest much of their own or the Church's money in an endeavour to realise the hope? That, after all, is the great test of sincerity.

CHAPTER II

OF CERTAIN CAUSES THAT JUSTIFY WAR

1. *GERMAN Invasion of Belgium.*—War, I take it, should not be declared without cause: may, that is, be waged only in defence of a nation's right; nor is it justified by every slight injury. Moreover, the deadlier the struggle is likely to be, the greater is the cause required. All this is evident.

Among the ethical questions raised by the late war was this: whether a belligerent nation that wishes to send an army through the territory of a neighbouring state, has a right of transit; which, if refused, may be enforced by arms. The Germans did this, in regard to Belgium; but, to give them their due, their politicians seem to have admitted that this invasion was not justified merely by necessity. At first they confessed they did wrong, but would make amends in time. Then they maintained that the Belgian Government had violated their rights, in permitting, or engaging to permit, French or English troops to pass in the same circumstances. Some even asserted that the French did actually pass. Certain Catholic theologians of the Fatherland held, I grieve to say, that the invasion was justified by the mere necessity; while, at home, some of our own people would have liked to say the same; and did so, at first; but the injury was too manifest.

2. *The Principle.*—Were it not for the peculiar geographical position of Belgium,—between three of the belligerents: Germany, France, and England,—I should not object to the German claim—for facilities. A nation, as I shall have to point out, has certain claims on its neighbours; and may insist on them,—using force to secure them; the amount of force to be proportionate to the necessity.

It is, I fancy, something like the relations between individual landholders. One has no permanent right of way through the farm or estate of another; but having, on occasion, pressing need, he asks leave to pass. if it is refused, and the need is pressing, he passes without it; and therein is right. Should the neighbour resist, he may be pushed aside; as gently, of course, as possible; but even with a good fall or blow, if such is necessary and the need of passage is great. Where life is jeopardised, one is not bound to pay nice attention to the petty rights of churls.

The true obstacle to the passage of German troops through Belgian territory was not so much any right of the Belgians, as that of France and England; for whom it was no less necessary that the Germans should not pass. One cannot be simultaneously bound to contradictions—to let one pass and not to let; so the Germans,—who, in other circumstances might have claim enough,—in these had none. I abstract, deliberately, from international law and the treaties involved; which I leave to those who have knowledge of such matters.

3. *Anticipating Aggression.*—Some German publicists claimed, I believe, that their armies merely anticipated an attack by Belgium; as to the truth of which I express no opinion. My concern is with the principle: that if you have good reason to anticipate attack, you may "do it first", as David Harum advises. Only do not anticipate too much: the future aggressor must not be strangled in the cradle.

I should not blame Austria, had she attacked Italy before that country was ready for war; which was pretty sure to come when she felt prepared. Neither should I blame the Allies, had they throttled Turks or Bulgarians, before either took the side which it was plain they were about to take. People have accused England and France of hypocrisy, inconsistency, and such, for that, while complaining of the German invasion of Belgium, they invaded Greece themselves; but the cases, surely, were not on a par. For, apart from the question whether the King of Greece or M. Venezelos truly represented that country, it seems plain that had the former not been throttled, he would have done as his neighbour, in Bulgaria;

and the Allies would have had to fight with Greece as an enemy. The same has to be proved,—and, I submit, has not been proved,—with regard to Belgium. These, however, are matters of fact, not of principle.

4. *The Boer War.*—As I understand the contention of the British Government in this case, it was that citizens of theirs, who owned much valuable property in the Transvaal, were not being fairly treated by the rulers of that country; and that there was no hope of improvement till a radical change was made in the system of electing those who held power in the Transvaal. And as this change, in turn, could not be secured without pressure, it remained to apply the pressure—by force of arms.

There was, and will be, difference of opinion as regards the facts; and no less as to the motives of the British: all of which are matters for history. Ethics—which is my department—is concerned only with the principle: whether, supposing the facts alleged, they would justify war; on the additional supposition that the abuses were really very serious. I have no doubt but that a nation is justified in taking up arms to protect the lives or property of its citizens in other lands; provided the interest therein imperilled is considerable. On this ground, all the Great Powers, some years ago, sent military contingents to China, to protect the lives and property of their subjects at a time of revolution. And they may well have been right ethically.

5. *The United States and Japan.*—It is well known that, some years ago, the Japanese felt aggrieved by certain restrictions placed on the emigration of their people to the United States; and that reprisals were threatened which might ultimately lead to War. If we are to believe some prophets, the matter is by no means settled, and the war is certain to come. The difficulty, I believe, is not so much with the United States Government, at Washington, as with the people of the Pacific Coast; who, though subject to the federal authorities, have interests and wills of their own.

Here, again, there is room for difference of opinion as to the facts: whether, for instance, Japanese and Chinese immigrants are undesirable. No reasonable man can dispute the right of a nation to keep out such—the unhealthy, who might propagate disease; the very poor, who may be also unfit for work; and malicious or wicked people, who may be a source of moral corruption. There may, of course, be other reasonable causes of exclusion.

How far these, or any of them, hold for Chinamen and Japanese, is a question of fact, with which I have little or no concern. If they did not, or do not, hold, to a considerable extent, the United States would not be justified in a policy of exclusion; and if the United States Government per-sisted, nevertheless, and the Japanese were seriously aggrieved, these would be justified in using what pressure they could command,— even that of war,—to secure the rights of their citizens. This, I fancy, is not disputed by the jurists of the United States.

6. *Protection of Missionaries.*—We have heard a good deal of the protection of Christian missionaries in China; which many have denounced as—in great part, if not altogether—a cloak for greed and aggression. That also is a question of fact; and the same holds of Turkey.

There was once a Pope, I believe, who, finding that two kings, his spiritual children, were in danger of falling out and fighting, in their zeal to propagate the Gospel in a certain heathen country, made peace between them by drawing a line across the map of the region, and giving, as sphere of mis-sionary enterprise, what was north of the line to one, and to the other what was south; with a right, of which they availed, to support the missionaries, by armed forces, each in his own territory. We know what came of that, to the people who were portioned out—themselves and their lands and property.

Similarly, it has been alleged, by the English, that Adrian IV., himself an Englishman, commissioned their king to come over here and give peace and order to our distracted and demoralised country. And though some good historians have maintained that no such commission was given, with regard to Ireland, no one thinks of questioning the existence of the Bull on the ground that it would imply a departure from papal policy, or a denial of traditional papal doctrine. On the contrary, every canonist maintains that the Popes have a right, not only to send missionaries into heathen countries, but to authorise, and even compel, kings to support them therein by armed force. And the same applies to Christian kingdoms that are in need of reform.

7. *Spheres of Influence.*—It is not the Popes alone who would restore order in a neighbouring state; it is done even by the most democratic of republics. What happened in Cuba is of recent history: rebellion against Spain, fostered by a junta in New York, and largely endowed with United States money; not, of course, supplied by the Government, but only by subjects thereof. Then, when the disorder had lasted some time, an appeal to the United States Government to interfere; in the interest, partly, of humanity, and, in part, of the Union itself; the neighbour's house being on fire.

Something of the same kind happened in Mexico the other day; and should, they say, have happened sooner. It is what every nation does, and must do; even Bolshevist Russia cannot let its neighbours alone. There are hinterlands everywhere; regions where, indeed, we have no formal jurisdiction; but which, nevertheless, are within our sphere of influence— to see that no great disorder continues there. There can, I think, be no objection to the principle; though, of course, like that of protecting missionaries, it is liable to abuse, and has been abused greatly. It means the sending of military forces,— which means making war,—to secure the reign of order in a neighbouring state.

8. *The Monroe Doctrine.*—Perhaps the largest sphere of influence that has yet been claimed is that of the United States of America; whose declared policy it is that "the American continents are henceforth not to be considered as subjects for future colonisation by any European power"; as also that any interference on the part of any such power with any other people in either North or South America, "for the purpose of oppressing them or controlling their destiny in any other manner," will be regarded "as a manifestation of an unfriendly disposition towards the United States". This brings within the sphere of influence of the Washington Government whatever

is not directly subject to them in the whole of the American continent, North and South, with all the adjacent islands.

The claim, however immense, is the same in principle as is made by every Great Power with regard to its weaker neighbours; who cannot become subject to another Great Power without prejudice to the security of the nation to which at present they act as buffers. This seems not unreasonable, as regards an immediate neighbour; but whether it applies to the whole of a continent as large as North and South America, united, I am unable to decide.

9. *Missionaries of Commerce.*—We often hear of how England acquired her colonies, by robbery; as still, they say, she enlarges them. Wherein, of course, is some truth; for no conquest ever was made, nor empire extended, without accompanying injustice. I doubt, however, whether some of those who make this accusation against England have thought out the principle on which it is based. But apart even from any question of principle, it should, I fancy, make us hesitate either to make or to receive such a charge, if we would reflect that it lies against every state, even the most Catholic, that ever acquired a colony: Spain, for instance, Portugal, France.

We have seen how these, and others, were exhorted by the rulers of the Church to send missionaries to the heathen, as also to send armed forces to secure a hearing for the missionaries; and how this affected the great colonial possessions of Portugal and Spain. It is contended, however, that the nations of Europe have a right to trade with, as well as preach to, uncivilised peoples; who, moreover, though legitimate owners of the territories they occupy, do not hold them without some obligation to the human race at large. It is not to be supposed, for instance, that the Red Indian tribes, who showed little disposition for agriculture, had a right to keep uncultivated, as hunting grounds, the vast and fertile plains of North America. And when the ploughman's right, like that of the missionary, needed protection, armed forces were sent to give it; which meant seizing territory and founding the colonies of which complaint is made.

Then, again, consider how a colony, once established, extends, as it were, of necessity; given—what is sure to be—

lack of toleration, or peaceable neighbourliness, on the part of the bordering tribes; who, like those already ousted from the colony, are ill-disposed to give the settlers reasonable trade facilities. To read some diatribes against England, one would think the world would be much richer, happier, and more prosperous, if Columbus had not succeeded in reaching America, or if a white face never showed itself south of Assouan. The human race, in my opinion, has gained immensely as a result of both events; as has Egypt also, and Hindustan, by the English occupation. Whereby, nevertheless, is by no means implied that either Clive or Kitchener was quite immaculate; any more than Cortes was absolutely fair to Mexico or Pizarro to Peru.

10. *Self-Determination.*—We saw, in Part I. of this little book, how, like children in a family, a nation or a colony may, in the course of development, become entitled to increased self-control; either setting up for itself, as fully independent; or the people being allowed a greater share in the selection of their governors; or a minority, when of separate race from the majority, being allowed local self-government. These, I have said, are to be conceived as rights, which may be legitimately secured by pressure; provided this is not unduly severe.

Whatever may have been the tradition of the Catholic schools, the great practical world,—wherein, occasionally, high-placed Catholic churchmen have figured,—has shown, by its action, that it regarded the pressure of armed insurrection as not unduly severe, where it was really needed to assert some of these rights. Archbishop Langton, Primate of All England, was one of the leaders of the revolt that secured the Great Charter; and the Checo-Slovacs, in these latter times, have been led by Bishops. The Catholics of the United States of America do not yield to any of their fellow-citizens in the fervour with which they celebrate Independence Day; and were the Bishops to teach officially that there was no justification for the war whereby the Declaration of Independence was supported, who knows what would become of the Church in America?

It is not alone complete national independence, or the overthrow of a dynasty such as that of the Bourbons, Romanoffs,

Hapsburgs, or Hohenzollerns, that may, at the proper stage of national development, be compassed in this way, by force of arms; but even lower grades of self-determination—local government in whatever form or degree may be due to a people at the time. Few Catholic Irishmen, I fancy,—among either clergy or laity,—complain, on ethical grounds, of the conduct of the Volunteers in Grattan's time; though the very existence of that body was a menace of armed force against England, if she refused to grant the local self-government that Grattan and his supporters thought due to Ireland at the time. The same holds of the struggle of Hungary, under Kossuth.

Supposing, then, that Ireland is denied, at present, a degree of Home Rule to which she has a right; one could not object to the use of armed force to secure it, on the ground that the acquisition of mere local self-government could never justify an appeal to arms. The same, as far as I see, holds of the Volunteers of Ulster; whose threat of armed insurrection would be justified, if Home Rule for Ireland meant denial of such self-determination as is due to the Saxon Colony of the North-East. The question, however, demands a separate Chapter.

CHAPTER III

OF THE PRESSURE THAT MAY BE APPLIED TO
SECURE LOCAL SELF-GOVERNMENT

1. *THE Irish Volunteer Movement.*—In the later years of the Home Rule agitation in Ireland, there has been a new development; as the Anglo-Saxons of the north-east corner have openly proposed to take up arms, to oppose that measure. This has evoked a counter-demonstration on the same lines, from the rest of the country. Volunteers have been enrolled and drilled by both parties; arms have been provided; and on both sides men have proclaimed their determination to use these arms in defence of what they deem their rights.

2. *Extreme Demands.*—Extreme claims were made by both sides, at first. Ulster would have no Home Rule, for any part of the country; Nationalists would rule even in the north-east corner. The extravagance of these claims came, after a time, to be admitted generally. Ulster waived its objection to Home Rule, provided six counties of that province were allowed to rule themselves independently. The Irish Parliamentary Party agreed to this, as an experiment, for a time. And though they were taken to task for this complaisance,—by critics who were influenced by conflicting motives,—the country seemed to be settling down to accept the compromise; when the Nationalist volunteers got out of hand and broke into actual rebellion, no longer for Home Rule, but for complete independence.

3. *Principle of Armed Revolution Admitted by Statesmen.*—I do not think it necessary to discuss the hypothetical question whether, if Ireland were entitled to such independence, she could, given a fair chance of success, legitimately take up arms to assert her right. All Europe,—political Europe, at least,—now admits the

principle; which, moreover, has been acted upon and conse-
crated by Washington; who, in turn, but applied to his own
country what had been practically taught in England, in various
revolutions, from that of the Bishops and Barons under King
John, to that of the Puritans against Charles I., and that which
exiled James II. and brought William of Orange to the throne.

4. *Question as to Extent of the Principle.*—Supposing, however,
the present Government of Ireland to be legitimate; as, we have
seen, was and is the official teaching of the Catholic Church,
and as is proclaimed by Ulster Protestants; and supposing,
in addition, that, as I have been trying to prove, Ireland and
north-east Ulster each have a right to Home Rule, under a
central, Imperial Government; and supposing, further, that
this right were unreasonably denied; the question would arise
whether an ethic that justifies armed insurrection to secure
full independence, when due, would be as liberal if the right
asserted were merely Home Rule under a central, Imperial
Government.

5. *Two Points of Difference.*—The principle, you may say, is the
same in both cases: armed resistance in assertion of the right of
self-determination. There are, however, two points of difference.

In the first place, when a nation takes up arms to assert a
rightful claim to complete independence, it does not oppose
legitimate authority. For the acting government becomes a
usurper *ipso facto,* the moment independence becomes due.

Secondly, the justifying cause is less when it is only Home
Rule that is denied. People are not entitled to take up arms
against a legitimate government for every grievance, even
though it should be real. And it is conceivable, at least, that,
whereas denial of full independence, when due, would be
cause sufficient to justify insurrection, the same might not hold
for the lesser grievance of unreasonable denial of Home Rule.

6. *Non-Catholic Opinion Liberal.*—Nevertheless, I deem it likely
that the great body of non-Catholic opinion would regard
denial even of Home Rule as sufficient cause for armed insurrection. Sir Edward Carson seems to have been backed up in
England by the full strength of the Conservatives; while the
Liberal Government were afraid to appeal to the country

against him, lest he should be supported by a considerable number of their regular followers. Even the Radicals who would have supported Home Rule against Sir Edward, could not, I fancy, be depended on to do so, if they did not think his demand unreasonable, and his threat of armed resistance indefensible on that account. I doubt if they would have objected to the use of arms to defend a reasonable claim, for local government or Home Rule for Ulster. And what England thinks on a matter of this kind, may be presumed to be the feeling of non-Catholic countries generally.

7.—*Opinion of Irish Catholics.*—I do not know that Ireland is quite typical of countries that are Catholic; nor am I sure how Irish Catholics would regard armed resistance, to obtain Home Rule merely, supposing this to be due and yet unduly delayed.

The National Volunteers were enrolled, drilled, and armed, ostensibly to secure Home Rule. Against the Orangemen of Ulster, you may say; but not against the Government. It must, then, have been to aid the Government in its conflict with the Orangemen; for no Government could merely stand by and keep the ring for factions waging civil war. But if the Government were to defend a Home Rule measure against Orangemen, surely they could do so without aid of Irish Volunteers. I fear it is true that the enrolling and arming of Volunteers was intended to put pressure on the Government; so that those who supported the enrolling and drilling of that body, must have contemplated civil war as a means to secure Home Rule. But the Volunteers were supported, at first, by practically the whole of Catholic Ireland, lay and clerical.

Then, there was the movement against conscription; on the ground that Home Rule, which should have secured us our own choice in the matter, after the model of the colonies, was unduly delayed. Opposition to conscription, in the circumstances, was a kind of insurrection, to secure a special form of Home Rule. True, it was to be but passive resistance; which its conservative advocates took care to distinguish from recourse to arms, denouncing this as immoral. These conservatives, however, professed themselves determined to persevere in their resistance if the Government enforced the law; so that there must be conflicts and disturbance of all kinds, leading to God knows what. Not quite so bad, of course, as civil war; but still bad enough to raise doubts as to whether those who allowed the lesser evil, would not, when the pinch came, have to permit even the greater. The moderates among the Dublin Volunteers were dragged after the extremists in the rising of Easter 1916.

8. *Author's View.*—It may seem presumptuous, and something more, for an individual to harbour scruples as to what was, or might have been, sanctioned by such a body; still, I take it, we are free, not only to entertain a different opinion, but to give it expression. Taking advantage of this liberty, I presume, in all humility and reverence, to say that I cannot see my way to approve of any such active or passive resistance to a Government recognised as legitimate as would leave this exposed to be crushed by a powerful foreign enemy with whom it was engaged in a life-and-death struggle at the time. I would press it to grant any measure of Home Rule which I regarded as due, but not for more than was due; nor even for what was due would I allow any pressure that might seriously endanger the whole commonwealth.

It would, of course, be different, if the Imperial Union were not more necessary than Home Rule for those who applied the pressure. But in that case the whole supposition fails; for then the Government that is conceived to refuse Home Rule, would no longer be legitimate.

CHAPTER IV

OF THE CONDUCT OF WAR:
(I) OF BOMBARDMENT OF TOWNS,
AND OF REPRISALS

1. *THE Difficulty.*—On the supposition that war may be justly waged, there can be no scruple about killing those of the enemy who attack you—soldiers actually fighting or about to fight. They are aggressors; unjust, as we suppose; and therefore may be killed. It matters not that they are in good faith; as one may kill a lunatic, when there is no other way of saving oneself from his attack.

The difficulty about war arises from noncombatants; who suffer so much, in any case; many losing their lives. It is, no doubt, open to you to say that all who belong to the enemy nation co-operate in the unjust aggression, and so are liable to be killed. "The young men shall go to the battle,—it is their task to conquer; the married men shall forge arms, transport baggage and artillery, provide subsistence; the women shall work at soldiers' clothes, make tents, serve in the hospitals; the children shall scrape old linen into surgeon's lint; the aged men shall have themselves carried into public places, and there, by their words, excite the courage of the young, preach hatred to kings, and unity to the Republic". So wrote Barrère, in a Report that was afterwards embodied in a Decree, during the French Revolution; as may be seen in Carlyle.[1]

During the late war, everyone in the belligerent nations co-operated with the fighting men in some way. The ploughman who turned the glebe in Kerry, did so to grow potatoes or grain; which, if not sent to the British armies, served to feed

[1] *French Revolution*, III., B. Iv., Ch. vi.

those for whom Great Britain would have had to make provision otherwise. Your Kerry ploughman, therefore, was a belligerent; as surely,—though, perhaps, not so efficaciously or persistently,—as those who forged guns at Woolwich or Essen, or brought up shells to the batteries in the field.

2. *May Co-operators be Slain?*.—Something like this was urged in "The Tablet", in support of the view that it is in no way wrong to make air-raids on German towns. An Indian chief, it was argued, may be shot for attacking you; and why not the squaw who, in his tent, prepares his arrows; and his son, who is still too young to do more than carry the arrows from the tent to the fighting line? Why not, similarly, rain bombs on the women and children of Germany? We read this sort of reasoning in "The Tablet".

The conscience of mankind is against it. Even the ex-Kaiser, Wilhelm, after an air-raid on Frankfurt, was reported to have written to the Mayor, to condole with the citizens, and protest against the barbarism of dropping bombs on open towns. London was always represented by the Germans as a fortress; wherein women and children stayed at their peril, and might be killed with safe conscience. One does not know which was the more inconsistent: the Catholic publicist who would bomb German cities, in reprisal for air raids on London; or the Kaiser who ordered or sanctioned the London raids, but protested that Frankfurt should be spared. When the danger approached themselves, both showed the true conscience of the race.

I deem it an enormity to say that, because a ploughman helps to grow corn that may feed those who supply an army; or because his little daughter knits or darns his stockings, his wife prepares his food, or his baby sucks taxed sugar; any or all of them may be put to death for cooperation in unjust aggression. If that were so, the citizens even of neutral states would not escape liability.

Accordingly, the principle that one may kill an unjust aggressor can be extended to co-operators only on condition that the co-operation is proximate and considerable.

3. *Grade of Proximity Difficult to Determine.*—So understood, the principle, I admit, is indeterminate; nor do I see any definite

line whereat to draw the amount of co-operation that would or would not justify killing. Extreme cases are easily decided. You may, for instance, shell a train that is bringing supplies to the firing line; but may not kill the wife of the driver merely because in some far-off cottage she knits a comforter for her husband. You may drop bombs on the Works at Essen or the arsenal at Woolwich; but should spare the home of the miner who helps to supply these places with coal or steel.

How near either mineral must be to the war zone and actual aggression, no man can say—with mathematical determination. I should not object to the bombing of a munition train leaving Calais, or even Woolwich; but I do not think you would be justified in bombing a train that leaves some Welsh mine with coal destined ultimately for the British fleet. There must necessarily be a belt of disputable territory between the extremes of certainty—lawful or unlawful—in matters of this kind.

4. *May such Non-Combatants be Killed Indirectly?*—There is, however, another principle on which, perhaps, one might be justified in taking the life of that Kerry ploughman or that knitting woman: indirectly, as it is phrased. An airman drops a bomb on plough or cottage, as is his right; even though, with either, ploughman or housewife should be blown to pieces. Though sorry for their fate, duty to his country requires the airman to proceed; to bomb the next cottage or plough, with whoever may, unfortunately, be near. You would not forbid a commander to fire on a fortress, even though some women or children should be killed therein.

I would not; and yet I would not allow him to fire on that plough, lest he should kill the ploughman; even though he might smash it to his heart's content, were there no danger for the man. There must be some proportion, between the good you attain and the evil you do in attaining it; as also between the chances or danger of doing either. If an apple were so placed as, if shot at, to endanger merely a pane of glass, even an unskilled archer might take the risk; but, on the head of a child, it needed all the skill of Tell to justify the bowman. You may run down and kill a man to save your life, but not to save a trifling sum of money. I cannot believe the slaughter

of a number of innocent London citizens justified by damage done to one of its railway termini: with the seat of war in
Eastern France.

5. *Air-Raids and Long-Range Guns.*—Those who drop bombs
on cities, from air-ships or aeroplanes, are often not justified in
doing so, even though they aim at some arsenal or other legitimate object of attack; for lack of proportion between the good
and evil they are likely to do. Allow that the action would be
right, if the airman was certain to hit the arsenal, or even if he
had anything like a good chance of success. Often, however,
they are up so high that, what with the rapidity of their motion,
there is little or no chance of their hitting anything in particular beneath; and it takes a good deal to justify this. I do not
say that it is never justifiable; if you suppose the good in view
to be very great indeed, and the non-combatant population
underneath sparse; as it often is, near the front lines, where
the probability of injury is proportionately small.

The same applies to bombardment with long-range guns,
such as the Germans used against Paris. It is out of question,
manifestly, to direct a shell from such great distances,—
seventy miles or more,—so that there would be any real hope
of injuring a combatant, or gun, or fort, or some one who, as
proximate co-operator in the war, may be killed on that
account. The most you can do is hit the city somewhere; with
the practical certainty of taking innocent lives. Catholic ethics
does not allow this, as I understand the science.

6. *Reprisals.*—When London and other English towns were
being bombarded from the air, with no little loss of life and
limb to the non-combatant citizens, a number of public men
advocated reprisals in kind, as the only effectual way of bringing the Germans to anything like a sense of the wickedness of
their conduct. The French, I understand, threatened reprisals
from the beginning; and carried out the threat. In time the
English followed; claiming, as a rule, to direct their bombs
only at legitimate objects of attack; but, it is to be feared, letting
them fall at times from heights at which it was impossible to
give them any such direction. Others advocated slaughter of
non-combatants by way of reprisal for the delight that was

shown, as reported, even by the women of Germany, at the destruction wrought by the air-raids on English cities.

Here, again, it is not for ethical science to adjudicate on the fact—whether and how far the Germans rejoiced in this way. Let us suppose they did. The real question is, how proximately they co-operated thereby in the raids, or in others that might follow. Was it so proximate as to justify the English in killing those German women, as unjust aggressors?

I find it hard to believe it; so that, in my opinion, neither the women of Germany nor the non-combatant men,—nor, above all, the children,—could be killed on that score. Reprisal, therefore, was unlawful, in so far as it meant killing such people by any shot or bomb that would not be otherwise justified.

It was hard, no doubt, on the French and English; but so it would be if one's home were attacked and one's wife and children slain, by an armed band of robbers. Kill them, in punishment, if you can; but it were barbarous, surely, if, when you cannot reach the murderers themselves, you make it even with them by killing their wives and children. This could not but bring counter-reprisals; and not only morality but civilisation would collapse.

7. *Prisoners, Spies, Traitors, Cowards, and Deserters.*—Enemy soldiers may be killed, as aggressors; but only when actually attacking or preparing to attack; provided also you cannot save yourself by disarming and imprisoning them. Captured and disarmed, their lives must be spared. It is part of the natural law; which, on the supposition,—now universally admitted,—that their attack was made in good faith, does not allow one to put them to death in punishment of an assault which was only materially sinful. All Catholics, I fancy, would agree on this.

But, then, what about spies; who, when disarmed, are shot unmercifully, though no one deems their faith less good than that of the soldiers in the open field? The leaders, also, in the Irish revolution were shot,—as men in like case would have been shot by any other government,—for treason; which, however they may have been guilty objectively, they surely committed in good faith.

Then there are cowards. An officer in the British Army,—
a most humane and just man,—told me of how by far the
most repugnant of all the duties he had to perform was to
shoot with his own revolver, in the trenches, men who were
writhing in a paroxysm of fear. Poor fellows, surely they could
not be formally responsible! Nor deserters; at least in many
cases: where they do not leave an important post defenceless;
nor sometimes even then. All these are shot without scruple,
in every army in the world. Can it be that there are circumstances wherein one may be justly punished with death even
for an offence committed in good faith?

I find it hard to believe it; though the universal practice is
undeniable, and it is scarcely less hard to ascribe this to
undeveloped moral sense. Yet I am disposed to regard this as
the more likely alternative; and to hope for a time when captured spies will be treated like other prisoners of war; honest
revolutionists likewise; and when cowards and deserters will be
so much pitied that they will not be put to death. We have
reached the stage when those who have been convicted of
political offences get special treatment, when imprisoned; for
which I see no reason but a recognition that offences such as
theirs are usually committed in good faith. Governments were
not always so tolerant. Is it too much to expect them to show
like toleration to spies and others, who, as the governments
themselves would be the first to recognise, are most likely to
have acted with the best intentions? May we hope for a time
when leaders in unsuccessful revolution will not be put to death?

CHAPTER V

OF THE CONDUCT OF WAR: (2) OF BLOCKADE

1. *ETHICS of Blockade.*—From time immemorial it has been held right to blockade fortresses, allowing no supply to enter, so that ultimately the garrison must either starve or surrender; and this even though great numbers of non-combatants, including women and children, would have to share their fate. It is hard to believe that this was wrong *securus judicat orbis terrarum.* The Germans, who complained latterly of the English blockade of their Country, had themselves no scruples about starving Paris into capitulation; nor, I take it, would they have hesitated to repeat the process in the late war, if they could.

It would, I have no doubt, be wrong to treat an enemy town in that way, if it did not contain sufficient combatants to justify the treatment. These the besiegers are entitled to kill, as unjust aggressors; while, as regards others,—non-combatants,—they must share the fate of the garrison. It is impossible to starve the aggressors, if you allow supplies to pass in for those whom you may not starve for anything they do themselves.

The garrison, no doubt, is forced, as a rule, to capitulate the sooner for the number of civilians that have to be provided for, or that die within the fortress for lack of provisions. It would be at least materially unlawful to drive these in by force, so that the place might have to capitulate the sooner and surer; making the deaths of these non-combatants a means to secure the surrender of the garrison. It has been done; and, I have no doubt, in good faith. Of that let God judge.

2. *Naval Blockade.*—"Blockading, in a naval sense, is the prevention of the entrance or exit of the enemy's ships at a

particular port, or at all the ports of a stretch of coast, so as to bring pressure to bear upon the inhabitants by obstructing their trade; and it renders intercourse with the enemy's ports unlawful on the part of neutrals".[1] The Atlantic coast of Germany was cut off in this way during the late war.

German statesmen and publicists complained of this; as if England acted inhumanly in starving their women and children. But few are disposed to credit the Germans themselves with consciences that would restrain them from doing the same thing to England, if they could. They did it to Paris without scruple, and very much more effectually; apparently even with satisfaction.

3. *Enemy Ships.*—Difficulties in this connection are raised during a naval blockade, when, as has been said, intercourse with the enemy ports is made unlawful for neutrals; who, as some contend, have a right to sail the sea and pass thereover anywhere. There has been, as is well known, no little controversy as to the provisions of international law on the matter.

I leave such controversies to the jurists; and deal only with the question in so far as it is governed by the natural law; which, no doubt, gives everyone a right of free passage over the seas; with certain limitations.

A belligerent, in the first place, can hardly complain if the enemy treat him on sea as on land, and as he treats the enemy. Those who either fight or minister proximately to the combatants are killed, where possible, as unjust aggressors; whether on sea or on land. Warships, therefore, and transports—used principally for the carriage of fighting men and of munitions—are sunk, just as soldiers are killed; either, of course, being merely captured and kept out of the way of doing harm, when they surrender.

Merchant ships also are treated just like merchandise found on land—captured or destroyed by the enemy, where possible. The crews, however, not being combatants nor ministering proximately to the combat, may not be killed as unjust aggressors; any more than those who work in the enemy's fields or

---

[1] *Chambers's Encyclopaedia*, art. "Blockade."

ordinary factories—not making munitions. You may take them prisoners, but must spare their lives. That is, if they do not resist, nor refuse to comply with orders. Otherwise, they would be unjust aggressors, if they resisted; or would be liable to punishment, if merely disobedient; and could be put to death on that account.

4. *Neutrals Trading with Enemy Ports.*—It is another question whether neutrals lose their right of free passage over the sea, when they do this to bring supplies to a port which a belligerent enemy has blockaded. To assert a right of passage to such a port is equivalent to denying the belligerent's right to blockade it; a right—that of blockade—which has been exercised by almost every nation, in every age; and which seems unquestionable.

Accordingly, the right of free passage over the sea is limited; provided you do not thereby make void the right of another—to blockade his enemy. The limitation seems reasonable; and therefore part of the natural law.

5. *Blockade Must be Effective.*—Maritime nations, however, while recognising this natural right of naval blockade, have insisted that it also is conditioned: that it does not hold where the blockade is not effective, in the sense of excluding sea-borne goods from the blockaded regions. Not that any blockade can be so effective as to exclude all passage whatsoever; as even from Paris, when besieged by the Germans, Gambetta escaped in a balloon. During the American civil war, also, the blockade of the Atlantic coast of the South, which the North held to be effective, was often run by English ships. There must, however, be no passage except by chance and stealth; and none at all without great risk of capture.

This also I regard as a provision of natural law; as otherwise Japan, for instance, could blockade the Atlantic coast of the United States merely by declaring it blockaded, without having one ship at command to see that the decree was observed. It would be an arbitrary and unnatural, and therefore illegitimate, restriction of the rights, let us say, of Germany or England, to trade with the United States. As well claim the right to forbid neutrals to send provisions or munitions to a city like Paris or Berlin, without taking measures to secure the isolation of the place.

6. *Mutual Trade of Neutrals: Freedom of the Seas.*—During the late war there was no little grumbling against England, on the part of the United States, Holland, and the Scandinavian peoples, because the British stretched the blockade of Germany so far as to prevent ships from carrying goods freely from the United States to the other countries just mentioned; or, conversely, from these to the United States. It was held that, however England might be entitled to prevent them from trading directly with Germany, she had no right to restrict their trade with one another.

The British did not interfere in that way at first; fearing, possibly, to antagonise those countries, and especially the United States, in which there was a large and active pro-German element. Nor was there any ground for the complaint after the United States declared war; seeing that the Government of that country then took care that not enough was shipped to Holland and the Scandinavian kingdoms to enable them to share with Germany. Before this happened, however, and as the war went on, the British thought that, despite their blockade, Germany was drawing supplies indirectly from the United States through Holland and the Scandinavians; and they,—the British,—claiming that this was an infringement of their rights, insisted that these countries should import from the United States no more than was necessary for the use of their own people. To secure this, the British fleet stopped and searched ships plying between these neutrals, and confiscated any supplies which they regarded as destined for German use. This, it was said, was denying neutrals the freedom of the seas.

The British reply was obvious: that, whilst they made no claim to interfere with the trade of neutrals with one another, as long as the goods transported did not pass to or from Germany; they did claim the right of interfering with German trade, even when carried under neutral flags. As regards the fact,—that such trade was being carried on,—they maintained that the evidence was amply sufficient to justify them in searching those neutral ships; after which, they undertook to make compensation for loss accruing, in all cases where the search showed that the cargo was legitimate.

Two questions, accordingly, came into dispute; first, one of principle: whether a United States merchant, though not allowed to trade with Germany directly, might do so indirectly, through a corresponding house in Holland or Sweden; and, secondly: whether, on the supposition that such indirect trade was illegitimate, during the blockade, there was sufficient evidence of the fact of its existence to justify the British in searching ships trading between those neutral countries.

I am not concerned with the question of fact as to which I believe the British contention well-founded. That, however, is only the opinion of a reader of newspapers—mostly of one colour. The New York, Dutch, and Swedish merchants may have been belied; or, if not on this occasion, others of their type may be belied next time; when, if there is no reasonable ground for suspecting them, it will be wrong to interfere with their legitimate trade.

With the question of principle I am concerned formally, as belonging to natural ethics; nor can I see how it may be answered reasonably otherwise than in the negative. Hold, if you can, that New York merchants were entitled to trade directly with Hamburg; so that any blockade that prevented them was an interference with their rights, and could not be tolerated by the United States. But it is unreasonable to hold that, while they might not trade with Germany directly, they could do so through Holland or Sweden. One is really as much German trade as the other.

I have heard it argued that, though England might reasonably complain of this, her remonstrance should be addressed to the government of the intermediary—Dutch or Swedish; but that the United States were not in fault, and could rightly defend their ships from search. But, surely, supposing the trade illegitimate, it would be as much the fault of the exporting house in New York as of the importers at Rotterdam or Gottenburg.

CHAPTER VI

OF THE CONDUCT OF WAR:
(3) OF THE SUBMARINE

1. *APART from Blockade.*—In previous naval wars it had been the custom,—if it was not even part of the international law,—for warships, when they fell in with a merchantman sailing under an enemy flag, to command her to stop; and, if she obeyed, to board, and take her, if they could, to one of their own ports; or, failing this, to take the crew and sink the ship and cargo. This supposed the merchantman to be unable to defend herself; as would usually be the case, if the warship were a surface craft.

Submarines, however, when on the surface, being easily sunk even by light guns, were in no position to approach and board merchantmen, so as to take their crews; as the merchantmen came to be armed for defence, and could sink a submarine when on the surface. Hence the Germans;—whose surface warships were all swept off the open seas, where they could only send submarines,—contended that these required a change in the customs or laws of war; so that, as they could not safely approach a merchantman, to secure her crew and passengers, if any; they might torpedo her without warning, leaving crew and passengers to save themselves by their boats, as best they could. In case the merchantman was unarmed, or that, for any reason, the submarine could speak her safely, her crew and passengers would be taken prisoners, or told to leave in their boats, before the ship was sunk.

As against this, the British held that it was wrong to fire on non-combatants; or, what was quite as bad for them, to make them betake themselves to small, open boats, often in a wild sea, when it was almost impossible to launch such craft safely from a lofty ship; and when, even though launched in safety, the human freight they bore could have little hope of reaching land. You may not, the British argued, kill such noncombatants by shooting them; but you kill them as surely by torpedoing their ship without warning, or even by ordering them into boats unless, indeed, the sea were calm and they were not far from land.

Here, again, I think, the conscience of the civilised world will support the English contention. For it is a question of killing those who, though belonging to an enemy country, are not guilty of any such act of aggression, or proximate co-operation with aggression, as would deprive them of the right to life. We have seen[1] that you may not shoot a ploughman, on the ground that he belongs to a hostile nation and helps to produce the food whereby it is enabled to attack you; nor may you bomb his cottage and slay his wife and children, on the ground that they co-operate in their way. There must be a certain proximity and degree of co-operation, to justify you in taking their lives. The same principle applies here, with regard to merchant seamen; whom you must not shoot or drown, unless the freight they carry should be closely connected with some attack on yourself; to the success of which, moreover, it should contribute in no small measure. It is not wrong to fire on a transport that carries soldiers, or munitions, to the field; just as one may bomb a railway train that brings supplies to the trenches.

You will object, perhaps, that it is only the ship which you attack directly; and that it is indirectly,—as being With the ship,—crew and passengers are killed. But it makes little matter. To justify one in sinking a ship in which there are innocent lives, she must be not only cooperating in the war, but doing so, at the time proximately and with considerable efficacy; and the more innocent lives she carries, the closer and more efficacious must her co-operation be. You may not sink a fishing boat and drown her crew, merely because they

[1] *Supra*, Part II., Ch. iv., Sec. 2.

supply herring to an enemy town wherein shells are made;
any more than you can throw at a ploughman's horses a
bomb which is liable to kill the driver as well.

2. *Cases in Point: Fishing Boats and Hospital Ships.*—Here,
again, there are cases wherein the ethical rule is plain; as also
a disputed area. I should deem it plainly opposed to the natural
law to sink fishing boats engaged in their humble business; as
also hospital ships, whereon are wounded soldiers. Some of
these, it is true, may recover and take the field again; but just
now they are non-combatants; and the ship on which they are,
though, no doubt, co-operating in the war, does not co-operate
so closely and efficiently as to justify the enemy in sinking her
while bearing their innocent lives.

The Germans, I fancy, admitted this, when they justified
their sinking of hospital ships on the ground that they were
used as transports—for combatants and munitions. While, as
regards fishing boats, they would contend, I suppose, that the
British fleet drew to no small extent on them and their crews.
As if you could bomb an open town merely because it contained a number of men who might be called to the colours.

All merchantmen, it seems to me, come under the same
rule, as long as they serve merely to carry food and such
necessaries to non-combatants at home; and do not act as
transports, to bring reinforcements, of troops or munitions, to
the armies in the field. Such ships are like the ordinary instru-
ments of civilian work on land—the plough, railway train,
mill,—which, as we have seen, may not be bombed with loss
of human life.

When a merchantman,—belonging to a belligerent,—carries
troops or munitions of war together with ordinary merchandise
and civilian passengers, the ethics of the case will not always
be so clear. To my mind, it varies—with the proportion of
civilian to military passengers, and of ordinary freight to
munitions of war; as also with the greater or less degree of
proximity wherewith the munitions carried may contribute to
the enemy's success. As no one, I fancy, would blame a German
warship for sinking a transport that was carrying troops or
munitions from Portsmouth to France, even though a few

civilians happened to be on board; so, I think, no one would exempt them from blame if they fired on an ordinary passenger ship or collier, even though it might be conveying a soldier or two, home on furlough, or a few cylinders of steel for Armstrong's or Woolwich. That is, on the supposition that there is no blockade.

3. *The "Lusitania" and the "Leinster"*.—The sinking of these two ships,—and especially of the former,—with the loss of so many innocent lives, horrified the world; including those who,—even in Ireland,—refused to see that those who torpedoed them committed any fault. This apart altogether from any right accruing from the attempted German blockade. The "Lusitania", it was said, carried shells, and possibly guns, for the Allied armies in France; while a number of soldiers were among the passengers on the "Leinster". By concealing, or striving to conceal, these facts, the British Government, it was said, recognised that they were likely to raise doubts as to whether there was not cause sufficient to justify the destruction of the vessels.

I agree that such an effort at concealment, if true, would show lack of conviction of some kind; though, possibly, lack of faith in the public conscience—whether, that is, it might not be affected by excuses or palliations based on the facts concealed. Catholics do not admit lack of conviction as to the truths of their faith, when they forbid publication of arguments that might tend to disturb it. With all this I am not much concerned; but only with this question of principle: whether ships engaged in ordinary commerce, may be destroyed, with loss of hundreds of civilian lives, merely because, in addition to civilians and common merchandise, they carry soldiers or munitions destined ultimately for the front.

I do not say that it is wrong absolutely—so that it could in no case be justified. If, indeed, the result of the war, or even of some considerable military operation, depended on the destruction of that consignment of troops or munitions, I should not blame an enemy commander for destroying them, even though, with them, others—non-combatants—were to lose their lives. As, however, in the cases before us, of the

"Lusitania" and the "Leinster"; so great a number of innocent lives were lost, Without appreciably diminishing the force of the assault on Germany, I find it hard to believe the killing of so many innocent people justified by a good result so paltry. This, again, apart from any complications that may arise from the question of blockade.

Neither vessel, it must be remembered, was a warship or military transport. Both were plying in the ordinary way of merchantmen; being used,—if, indeed, they were so used,— either by the British Government or those who supplied it, for purposes ultimately connected with the war. If it was grain or tinned meat that was being carried, for the ordinary public as well as for the army; or if the ships were sunk because they carried a number of men, hitherto unenlisted, who might, later on, be drafted to the colours; few, I fancy, would justify the sinking—apart from the rights of blockade. Were the shells in the "Lusitania", or the soldiers in the "Leinster", of sufficient importance to justify, by their destruction, that of the hundreds of innocent folk who perished with them; travelling, not on any warship, but on vessels engaged in the ordinary passenger trade? I do not believe the justification sufficient.

4. *The German Blockade.*—It was admitted by all that the German fleet had the same right to blockade England and France as England had to blockade Germany; but the Allies contended (1) that the German blockade was null and void, as being substantially inefficient; and (2) that, however efficient it might become, it could never be justifiable to sink without warning, or otherwise expose to peril of life, those who might be running the blockade, even illegitimately. That is, of course, if they did not resist the blockaders, nor try to escape when called on to surrender.

(1) It must, I fancy, be admitted now, even by the Germans, that their blockade was inefficient. Not only did they not prevent a constant mighty stream of supplies and reinforcements from crossing the English Channel; but the British were able to supply and reinforce armies in Greece, Palestine, and Mesopotamia; while, towards the end of the war, great bodies of troops, with plentiful supplies of all kinds, came across the

Atlantic. In English ports, moreover, general merchandise was unloaded every week in hundreds of cargoes. A blockade that could not prevent this was not efficient in any sense. And bear in mind, moreover, that if the contention holds that is here advanced, the rights accruing from blockade are conditioned by efficiency even under the natural law.

(2) The second part of the British contention,—that vessels such as submarines may not sink merchantmen without warning, and without allowing means of escape to the crews and passengers,—is more open to dispute. For the English view it is urged that blockade-running, though illegitimate, is not so grave a disorder as fighting with lethal weapons; for which reason those who merely run a blockade may not, like combatant soldiers, be killed as unjust aggressors. To which the answer,—a not unfair one,—is that it might be so if the blockade-runner was not armed for defence against submarines, by sinking them.

It will have to be admitted, I think, that a blockade may be legitimately conducted by submarines sinking at sight, provided that in this way they can make the blockade substantially efficient,

5. *The "Lusitania" and "Leinster" again.*—Accordingly, the true basis of complaint against the German navy is, not that they sank such ships as these,—which they could have done legitimately, had their blockade been efficient,—but that they sank them, with immense loss of innocent lives, while the vessels were on what should have been to them a free passage over sea, with liability, at the most, to capture. Had there been an efficient blockade, either the passage would not have been attempted, or, if attempted, those who dared it would be responsible for the loss. Travelling as they were, in the exercise of their right, the blame of their death falls on those who attacked them.

6. *Successive Efficiency.*—It will be said, probably, that a submarine blockade like that of the Germans, though inefficacious at any one time, may be truly efficient in ultimately sinking all merchantmen belonging to the blockaded country; as also those of neutrals who trade therewith; as Germany would

have done in the late war, had she had in the early days a sufficient number of submarines. If she had them, she would have been justified in sinking at sight, even though, for two or three years or more, she might not have prevented a diminishing number of ships from making and leaving the ports of England. And in the next war,—when, possibly, she may have provided submarines in sufficient number, not to sweep the seas of commerce with England at once; but to do it in one, two, or more years,—she will be justified in proclaiming such a blockade and enforcing it by sinking at sight. As, conversely, England will be entitled to do with Germany or the United States. All, of course, on the supposition that submarine blockade is not regulated meanwhile by international law.

I have the greatest doubts as to whether such a blockade, even though sure to prove efficacious ultimately, justifies a belligerent in killing for violation of it, before it has become effective. It seems to me that, till it has become effective actually, the sea is open, with a right of way for neutral vessels; who would suffer injury if sunk for exercising that right. As an illustration in point, it may be argued that a German airman could not legitimately drop bombs on a waggon carrying food into Paris, on the ground that, though the German army has not yet blockaded that city, they will have it completely surrounded by next year or the year after. Until it has been cut off actually, non-combatants from the country round, as well as neutrals from Spain or Switzerland, are within their right in supplying the city with food.

CHAPTER VII

OF SOME CONSEQUENCES OF WAR

1. *SOCIALIST Formula.*—Proposals were made repeatedly, during the war, for a conference of non-combatants,—Socialists, for the most part,—from both sides, at Stockholm or some other neutral city; where they might possibly agree on terms of peace; which, then, by force of moral persuasion, or even by strikes, would be imposed on the belligerent governments. There is some reason to regard the secret springs of this campaign as having been worked from Germany; while, in the open, the lead was taken by the Socialists of Russia, who propounded the formula: No annexations, no penal clauses in the peace treaty, and no indemnities.

This cry was so often repeated,—in so many speeches and newspaper articles,—that it came to be regarded as a kind of axiom; as if the natural law forbade annexation, punishment, or indemnity. It was said to be the one way to prevent future wars; and so commended itself to a certain class of humanitarians, whose eyes are "tender over drowning flies": product characteristic of a civilisation growing effete.

2. *Penalties and Indemnities.*—When your purse has been stolen, or your dwelling burnt, it is, no doubt, the better way to let the thief or burner have his freedom, instead of reporting him to the police. It is better, that is, for individuals, here and there; but I hope we are not bound to hold that it would be best also for society, constituted as it is, if the practice were made obligatory. Few, I suspect, would care to belong to a city or State wherein were no police; not because there was nothing for them to do, but because people would not have them do

it; deeming it necessary to let rogues and malefactors of all kinds have their way.

For the world, as it is, the safe rule is to insist on rights; not too rigidly, if you will; but yet to insist, so as to restrain injustice. If some one has stolen your property, make him restore it; should he have injured or destroyed it, require him to make good the damage. That is found, in practice, to be the most effectual way to preserve equal rights in this very imperfect world.

And as it is with individuals, so with nations; which experience, or history, shows to have a tendency to mischief, that is best kept in check by a consciousness, realised by experience, that damage caused unjustly will have to be made good. The cry now is to make the world safe for democracy; which can hardly be hoped for if, when tempted to attack, nations feel that, in case they fail, they will not be made amenable. High-minded folk, I know, arc compelled by their very nobility to be all the more generous in such circumstances; and perhaps democracies may come to that in time. One does not like, however, to trust them at the present stage of their development. Did not German Socialists vote supplies for the attack on Belgium? They may have more hesitation next time, if they find that the last raid, not only did not pay, but was expensive.

I refrain from emphasising the righteousness of punishment for the crime of unjust war, merely as punishment, and apart from any notion of reparation or of prevention of the same offence in future; though punishment, regarded purely as such, is justified by the Catholic tradition of ethics. The punishment of sin, we hold, will last for ever: therefore after it can possibly act as a preventive.

If I abstain from emphasising this in relation to war, it is because modern Liberalism, influenced in this country largely by J. S Mill, justifies punishment, in the case of man as of animals, solely on grounds of its preventive value. Let it be so; provided the punishment is allowed, and not unduly diminished, to the prejudice of the future.

3. *Unjust War Waged in Good Faith.*—It is a principle of commutative justice, as understood in Catholic schools, that

one is not bound to repair any damage one may have done in good faith, however unjust it may have been objectively; until, at least, one has been called upon to make good, by a judge or other superior holding supreme dominion. Nations however, are subject to no such superior; while few, I take it, would now be disposed to question the fact that wars, however unjust objectively, are declared and conducted in good faith, as a rule. So that, unless where bad faith is admitted,—as, perhaps, in the case of the German invasion of Belgium,— there does not seem to be any reparation due, or any claim for indemnity.

It would be a satisfactory reply to this if we could hold, with some able moralists, that a fault which is merely juridical,— supposing objective injustice or negligence merely, without bad faith,—is sufficient to found a claim to restitution. Such, however, is not the common opinion.

Perhaps we could fall back on Mill's view; that for such damage, wrought in good faith, reparation may be exacted, not as punishment, for an offence completely past, but in the way of prevention; as one beats a dog or horse, to supply a motive for better conduct next time. Such penalties are exacted from children and irrational animals, even though the faults we find in them, and which we want them to avoid in future, have been committed in good faith. Why not deal with nations in the same way? They do not belong to us, no doubt; but they are supposed to have injured us, and to be capable of doing so again. May not this give us a right to supply them with sufficient motives not to interfere next time with our rights?

May not nature, moreover, which sanctions prescription between nations, allow this right of punishment for juridical offences, as necessary for self-protection?

4. *Annexations.*—From the dawn of history it has been found that, when a nation has been conquered in war, the reparation or penalty exacted by the victor has been, in most cases, annexation of the whole or part of the territory of the vanquished. This, of course, was very often carried to excess, as a penalty, even where the victor nation had suffered injury; as was not always the case. But if we suppose the war just on

their part, so that they had a right to indemnity, it is hard to deny that there may be cases wherein the only possible mode of obtaining it is to take over territory from the conquered. The Catholic schools have always regarded this as legitimate.

Our predecessors went even so far as to hold that, in punishment of unjust war, the people of a nation might be reduced to slavery. And though we should not now authorise slavery, as found among the ancients, we allow it in the form in which it appears so commonly among ourselves—economic subjection, whereby people have to work, in straits, to supply good things for others. Payment of any debt may mean this, for individuals as well as nations.

5. *Annexation and Nationality.*—It is now contended, I understand, that reparation, however justly demanded, may in no case go so far as to interfere with nationhood: must, that is, always allow peoples of separate stock to govern themselves, in complete independence; or, at least, to remain associated with others of the same race, as parts of a self-ruling nation.

This, no doubt, is desirable; so that if a people can pay whatever indemnity may be due of them, without calling on anything but the chattels at their disposal, they should be allowed to pay in that way, remaining personally independent. But if, as may be, they have not wherewith to pay, apart from the land and what is fixed to the land; and if, as also may be, they do not want to give these, preferring to hold them even under the rule of a conqueror; who shall say that deprivation of national self-government would not be justified? At the time of the Cromwellian settlement in Ireland, many of those who were deprived of estates got an option of land in Connaught, but would have preferred to stay in their old homes, even as tenants of the new proprietors. They would, of course, have been much more willing to remain, if allowed to own the soil. Had the war been just on the part of Cromwell,—as is conceivable,—who shall say that he would not have been entitled to annex these estates, even though the conquered owners were Gaels and the conquerors Anglo-Saxon? Had the White Man no right to annex the territories of the American Indians, or of the Australian Bushmen; and with the territories

to reduce to subjection Indians and Bushmen themselves?
That is, on the supposition that the wars between these races
were just on the part of the Whites.

I make bold to assert that the whole trend of the tradition
of Catholic ethics is in favour of allowing annexation of people
vanquished in just war; even though previously independent
and of different stock from their conquerors. The tradition
goes even further; allowing such a nation, vanquished in just
war, to be reduced to slavery. Where any number of authorities might be quoted, I must confine myself to this, from
Cardinal De Lugo; who, amongst the grounds of slavery,
mentions in the first place the right of war. He proceeds:—
"This title extends even to infants captured in war; who,
though they may not be justly killed, may be made slaves. For
I take it, from the treatise on Laws, that penalties in external
goods of fortune may be inflicted on people even for the crimes
of those to whom they belong. Children of heretics, for instance,
or of those who have been guilty of high treason, suffer infamy,
by reason of their parents' crime. A conqueror, therefore, may
punish an enemy nation that he has conquered, by reducing it
to slavery; punishing it even in the infants that belong to it.
For as he may despoil such infants of their goods, as being part
of the enemy nation, so he may deprive them of liberty".[1]

1 know that this would be allowed no longer; and that, in
so far, I myself recognise the need of some modification of the
tradition. One should not, however, carry such reforms too
far; as do those Socialists who contend, apparently, that nations
should suffer no penalties whatever, even though they may
have been waging an unjust war. If there is to be punishment,
let it be adequate; as, it seems to me, it will not be, in certain
cases, unless the whole or part of the criminal republic,
though of different stock, is made subject to the people whom
they have injured. It is not desirable; but it may be necessary,
to prevent future aggression.

---

[1] *De Iustitia et Iure*, Disp. vi., n. 12.

APPENDIX

OF IRELAND SINCE THE UNION; AND OF THE PROSPERITY OF HOLLAND, DENMARK, AND OTHER SMALL NATIONS.

1. *AUTHOR'S Apology.*—In criticism of what has been said in Part I., as to the benefits accruing to Ireland from union with Great Britain, it will be said, I expect, that, whatever the advantage to the predominant partner, Ireland suffers. In proof of which critics point to her ever diminishing population and disappearing industries.

The argument proves, as it seems to me, that there has been and is something wrong; but I do not see that it can be no other than the Union. May it not be that the Union never got a fair chance; and that the way to such prosperity as is possible for people with our resources, lies, not in breaking away from England altogether and setting up a fully independent republic, but in modifying the terms of Union, and amending our own ways? Perhaps I should not touch on a question that does not belong to ethics so much as to politics or business of some kind; but may one not criticise, in this Appendix, some of the arguments in current use?

2. *Diminishing Population.*—In fairness to the Act of Union it should be said,—though, in this connection, it is heard rarely,—that for nearly half a century after it was passed the population of Ireland grew steadily. It was about 4,500,000 in 1800, and had risen to 8,500,000 in 1846; when it began to decline. Some new cause must have come into play when the fall began; which it is for criticism to determine.

There was, of course, the potato blight, which occasioned the famine; but, as famine ceased, though the blight has continued, I doubt whether this is the only or main cause of the decline of population. Besides those who died, we lost a couple of millions by emigration, in the black days; but it was not the potato blight that drove them away.

The year 1846 was remarkable for another event—the repeal of the Corn Laws; in itself more revolutionary than the famine, and symbol of a still greater revolution—that in trade. Steam had begun to show its power, in mine, mill, and road; producing goods in rapidly increasing quantities, and transporting them with ever-growing facility over land and sea. With the result that the urban population of England rapidly increased; well paid, and clamouring to be well fed.

Now the food for which they clamoured was mainly corn, meat, and butter; and corn just then, began to be produced in abundance oversea. It was then, remember, the Mississippi valley was being reduced to cultivation; itself a revolution and cause of revolutions. It grew cereals; but did not give meat, just yet. Russia also had plenty of corn ready to pour into the English markets, and needing only ships to carry it; which steam supplied. This abundance poured into England, at a low price, when the Corn Laws were repealed; with the result that growing corn ceased to pay in these islands.

Ireland, however, had been living by growing corn: living and paying rent thereby. How were we to meet this competition? So far no meat came, nor butter; and people foolishly hoped that these products could never come; so landlords, then all-powerful in Ireland, resolved to turn their fields into pasture and produce meat. This led to consolidation of holdings; with evictions from the rich lands; and something of the same kind in poorer soils, for the production of butter; the whole coming at a time when land was to be had for nothing in the Mississippi valley, gold could be picked up by Californian rivers, and one could get fabulous wages without going beyond New York. Low prices at home and abundance oversea,—this, not the potato blight, was the true cause of the stream of emigration that set out then from the shores of Ireland.

That revolution took place in Britain which profited by the Union, as well as in Ireland; with the single difference, that whereas British agricultural labourers got well-paid work at home, in the factories, while British farmers got a good market near them, the Irish had to go and send their produce oversea.

It was not the Union that caused either emigration or immigration; but the development of steam-power, with the opening up of so much new territory. Had we in Ireland been our own masters, we should have had to face the same problem, caused by the loss of our market for grain; and we should probably have found some more or less effectual remedy long before now.

It is the main argument for Home Rule; that, as the United Kingdom has been managed hitherto, by a single common Parliament at Westminster, Ireland did not get fair play. She should have had some power to meet emergencies such as we have been considering; power within herself, since the predominant partner was careless, thinking there was no emergency at all.

I do not see how it would have helped if we had been allowed to put a tariff on imported corn; unless it were put on corn imported into Great Britain, where our market had been; and, if we were completely independent, we could hardly expect to be allowed that.

In a country where agriculture was becoming uneconomic, as a result of competition, rents should have been reduced; and the landlords should not have been allowed to maintain the old, impossible burthen, by turning their estates into ranches, to the detriment of the common weal. In this way Ireland might, possibly, have been able to maintain her staple industry; and if, moreover, Imperial taxation had been made more equitable, and she had been allowed control of her local resources, she might have assisted the farmers in many ways; besides improving her fisheries; when both, no doubt, would have reacted on centres of manufacture. It has to be proved that much cannot be done in this way, even though we remain firmly and loyally united to Great Britain; taking advantage of our proximity to her markets, and doing our part to sustain and enlarge them. It could, I fancy, be proved more easily that much has been done, since the beginning of the Land Movement.

3. *Vanishing Industries.*—The Union, I submit, is still less to blame for the closing down of mills than for the decline of

agriculture; though here also the evil would have been met, to some extent, if not wholly, had there been less centralisation—had we been allowed local self-government. Certain facts, I fear, are commonly lost sight of, that should be borne in mind.

Belfast, in the first place, flourished mightily under the Union; without any special favour that I can discover. In 1800, when the Act was passed, the population of that city was but 20,000; now it is 400,000. It grew like any of the great towns of England, and by the operation of the same causes—application of the new energy, of coal, through the newest and best machinery: spinning-jenny, power-loom, and the rest.

The same holds of the other towns of Ulster, where factories rose and prospered: everywhere coal working through the newest and best type of machine.

In the rest of Ireland, I submit, it was different; or else, where it was not different, there, too, was success. In Kilkenny, for instance, which I know best, there had been considerable manufacture of woollens, starch, and leather; but the manufacturers continued to use old-world machines and methods; with the result that they were beaten in competition. The woollen mills, moreover, depended wholly on the water-power of the Nore; which, of a dry season, may be little more than a trickle, for weeks at a time. Ten miles away, at Castlecomer, they had some of the finest steam-coal in the world; but they lacked the brains, or the spirit, to turn it to account. Is it any wonder they went down?

One man of some business capacity bought the Ormonde Mills there,—a dying concern, with a splendid position,—installed some new machinery, and made it a success: nothing, of course, to what it might have been made. I saw it, after his death, managed by his daughter; who, girl as she was, improved on her father's position; thereby showing what could be done under the Union. The Mahonys and the Moroghs, in or near Cork, built up flourishing woollen mills, while those of Kilkenny were falling into decay.

So of our flour mills, the ruin of which is so often ascribed to the Union, while the true source of rot is to be found elsewhere. This industry, too, was revolutionised, by the introduction of the roller; with the result that those who continued to use stones could not compete. Where the new method was adopted, it made fortunes; even in Ireland, under the Union. The Bolands succeeded in Dublin, wonderfully; Mosses, Pilsworths, Brownes, in Co. Kilkenny; Shackletons, Odlums, and others, in the Midlands; Hallinans, Russells, Furlongs, Goings and Smiths, in the South; MacCanns, Pollexfens, elsewhere. Many of these did not even use steam-power; though, where this was adopted, as by the Bolands, the success was greatest.

When anyone tells me that the Union is responsible for the non-development, and even the decay, of Irish industries, I am wont to ask him, please, to tell me what law was passed, or not passed, by the Imperial Parliament, to keep the Suir from being as great a centre of industry as the Lagan; and I never hear of any. There—in the Suir—we have a noble river; tidal from the Tower of Hook to Carrick—a stretch of thirty miles or more; with the Barrow running northwards, no less fine and tidal, for twelve other miles. The two are as near the coal and iron of Wales as is Belfast to those of Scotland: why is not Waterford another Belfast? Why did the Vulcan Foundry, the Graving Dock, and the glass industry fail? Because, I suppose, they were not dry-nursed from the public exchequer: as if Harland and Wolfe's, or Goodbody's Jute works, or Jacob's biscuit factory, were fostered in that way.

We had at one time, at Portlaw, a cotton mill, in which I myself saw 2,500 hands at work; and there was a branch at Carrick. They were built by the Malcomsons,—not an Irish name,—who prospered greatly, even under the Union; till they, too, failed; having, I suppose, become more Irish than the Irish. Their failure, any way, was not due to the Union, under which they had flourished; and they failed in Britain no less than on the Suir.

The fact is, I fear; that we Gaels have not the business turn of mind, and so do not build factories even now, anywhere: on the banks of Hudson or Mississippi any more than on Suir or Liffey. We never built them—never were a commercial people. Mrs. Green, I know, has made a brave attempt to show the contrary; but the fact that our towns owe their origin to the Gall,—Dane or Norman-English;—that alone is decisive.

Even when Danes and Normans had shown us how and where to build and fortify cities, and to make use of river-mouths, and when commerce had begun to develop, very little of it, I fear, was in the hands of the Gael. Hence their weakness, as compared with the strangers depending for arms on doles from France, and Spain and "the Royal Pope." A race that despises trade, and will not fight for it, is pretty sure to be dependent.

We hoped that a new era had dawned: that our people were beginning to feel their way to real independence, through commerce. But while the Great Powers of the world were in death-grips, bleeding from every vein in the battle for trade; we looked on, pluming ourselves on the "spirit" that would not allow us to mix in such a squabble. We saw our only customer straitened and in imminent danger of being bled white; and we folded our arms, as if the result were no concern of ours;—those of us who did not rejoice in the wounds she received, and in the prospect of her approaching impoverishment. With the result that, now that she has saved her trade and ours,—if, indeed, she has saved it,—we go hat in hand to Mr. Wilson. And we call this self-reliance!

4. *Holland, Switzerland, and Scandinavia.*—When I say this, I am often told to look at Holland, Switzerland, and the Scandinavian kingdoms, and compare their lot with that of Belgium. Which would I have the Irish people share? Do not Holland and Denmark trade with England? Yet no one reproaches them, as fools or cowards, for not sharing her battle. What becomes them and suits their interests so well, should be good enough for us.

I am not asked to look at Wales or Scotland; who thought it their duty, and worth their while, to pour out treasure and blood to help England keep the common market. Which position is the more like ours—that of Denmark or of Scotland?

And a noble figure Scandinavian and Dutchman cut during the world-war; shivering at every movement of the

German sword-arm; and seeing their ships sunk ruthlessly, without daring to whisper more than a mock complaint! They grew rich by supplying the submarines that sank them; as did our farmers by feeding the English tyrant.

Had Germany won, there would have been a Central European Zollverein, taking in the Low Countries and Scandinavia. France and England having been bled white and reduced to impotence, Holland and Scandinavia would have had no market but Central Europe; where they would be at the mercy of the German merchants. They could join the Bund,—would, indeed, have to do so,—and thereby acknowledge themselves vassals; or if they were allowed to remain out, they would be all the more enslaved to the Central Powers. England and France fought for the commercial independence of Holland and Scandinavia; and these fed the German armies; as we prayed for their success and applauded them. When at last, Germany went down, and the sabre was wrenched from her grasp, Denmark mustered courage to put in her bill for Schleswig !

Yet for these countries it can be said that to them it mattered little how England fared; since, though she were beggared, they would have a market in Germany—at their doors. No doubt, the ports of Britain were free; whereas there was, and will be, a tariff on the German frontiers; unless, indeed, Holland and the rest should become German provinces. Germany, however; is near them—nearer than England; and they might hope to find a market there.

If the Scotch were to say all that, what would the world think? Yet they are nearer the German market than we, and ever so much keener business men.

That, accordingly, is what strikes me, when reminded thus of Scandinavia and Holland: which did not cut noble figures during the war; were not much more prudent than noble; and, in any case, are not in the same position as we—so deeply interested in the prosperity of Great Britain.

I have said before, that, during the Irish land war; certain farmers stood aloof, and profited by their neighbours' sacrifice; as do certain workmen in times of strike. We know what decent people think of and call such. Holland and Scandinavia, to my mind, were pretty much in that position.

If the Germans had won, and made Germany the only European market; and if, after some years, the United States were to attack Germany, with intent to take the market over the Atlantic; and if, in this new struggle, Germany was in imminent danger of defeat; it would be poltroonery and cowardice on the part of Holland and the Scandinavians to look on with arms folded. It would be lunacy on their part to rejoice in the prospect of defeat for Germany; and it would be suicidal to join in the attack on her.

5. *Independence.*—I have reproached the new Irish "soul" with going hat in hand to Mr. Wilson; whereas I myself would make terms with England, and the whole burthen of my teaching is, that, apart from her, we cannot stand. The balance, in the way of independence, seems to be against me.

But is there in an appeal to a comrade, to stand back to back with one against a common foe, nothing manlier than in a petition to a patron, to do all the fighting, or after he has done it, to share the fruits? Independence does not mean standing alone: the greatest cannot do that. It means keeping up your end; or defending your bit of trench, and so keeping the enemy from outflanking those to right and left of you; while they, in turn, defend your flanks.

There are circumstances wherein a man of spirit may beg,—Belisarius did it, they say,—but not when one can work. Were we in Ireland not in position to help ourselves, this appeal to Mr. Wilson might not argue lack of spirit. But if, as is here maintained, what we complain of now is nearly altogether due to lack of energy, skill, or grit on our part, this appeal to Mr. Wilson does not argue the kind of independence I want to see developed in my people. Self-help! but let it be ourselves, as much as possible.